I Am a Work in Progress

Joe Quieros BA(Hons), PGCE, Dip.Hyp. GHR. GHSC. NLP Cert. CPLR

The Behaviour Change Specialist

LIFE UNLIMITED HYPNOTHERAPY
Reframe, Refresh, Renew, Rise

ISBN: 978-1-3999-7405-9

DEDICATION

To my reasons for living – Elena, Francesca, Lily x
Never forget how loved you are, how intelligent, funny, caring,
fascinating and beautiful you are. You deserve to be happy and
fulfilled and to know your Mama is right beside you every step.
Thank you for all the joy you bring into my life as well as the
drama. You have taught me to be a better person and I hope I have
become the role model you needed x

Mama x

CONTENTS

ACKNOWLEDGMENTS

I am forever grateful for the lessons I have learned and the
personal growth and development I have gained.
I share with you here some of my personal story, knowledge and
tools that I have learned through study – I have credited where
necessary and would never intentionally claim certain ideas as my
own. I have written this book and the 12 practical tools, in
particular, in order to make them accessible to all.
Just as I have benefited, I hope to lighten your burden and give you
the tools to live your life unlimited.

PART ONE

REFRAME

1 SEE YOURSELF STEPPING FORWARD CONFIDENTLY

Imagine yourself stepping forward in life, in any situation, feeling confident and capable, unlimited by any self-doubt or fear. What purpose does that old fear have as you move forwards in your life? Do you see your goals as unachievable? What is clouding your view? If you have a dream, do you see it as achievable or out of reach? What makes you doubt your ability to attain it? Where does this self-doubt originate?

Who do you want to be? How do you want to see yourself? How do you want to feel about yourself? Personally, I want to be seen as capable, loving, warm, caring, intelligent, motivated, ambitious, adventurous, strong and successful. I take steps each day to reinforce this belief in myself or to enhance skills which I feel need extra definition. I study, I expand my knowledge, I set myself challenges, such as writing this book or creating workshops and retreats. I know that there are people who doubt me, who fear that I will fail but those are the voices to which I do not listen to. I know that they are people who love me and who want me to be happy and not hurt anymore. They want to keep me safe. They believe that by not venturing too far from the norms of society and playing it safe will keep me safe and happy. I know that this is limited thinking. I no longer want to play it safe. I am made for so much more. I am capable of so much more and each day, with each learning experience I have, I know more and gain more self-belief and courage. I am curious of what I can create and become.

There are other people who say I will fail. These people are not friends. These people are definitely not the voices I wish to listen to, knowing how their negativity comes from a low vibrational place. It spurs me on rather than deters me. This is because I have grown beyond them. I have outgrown my inner fears of insecurity and inferiority. I see them for who they are and what they are. I see me as separate. I have grown and worked on myself, and I have left these people in the past. When they say "you've changed" I say "Thank you. Yes, I have." I no longer accept or tolerate toxicity in my life. I am no longer needy or in search of validation through others. I know my worth. I am priceless! We all are. Just look closer – you will see how special you are. You will see how people try to limit you and how you have come to accept that. It is time to break free of those limiting ideas.

When you dream of your future, with regards your career or your personal life, do you dream small? Are you realistic or do you dream wildly and disproportionately? However wildly ambitious your dream may seem to you or others, remember that someone, somewhere has already achieved this. If they can do it so too, can you! Bear in mind that there needs to be realism in your goal, however. Ensure you follow the SMART goal technique to ensure success. Aim high but not over the rainbow. Maybe start with a smaller challenge and work your way up to the big dream. I struggle with this one – I am so excited and passionate to reach the ultimate dream that I have to stop and reign my enthusiasm back a little. Step by step, Joe!

It is by taking those steps that we will achieve our goals. Each little step you take towards it makes it that much more attainable - regardless of whatever limiting belief you have. So why allow those beliefs to continue?

You have achieved things in your life – look back honestly and with compassion and you will recall moments of success, courage and resilience. Write down instances of when you were brave; when you were successful; when you felt proud of yourself; when you overcame difficulty or opposition; Close your eyes and envision yourself back in each of those moments. Feel that pride and strength radiating throughout your body. Feel that excitement and pride again. Let it fill you and inspire you. If you have felt this success once, there is nothing to stop you from experiencing it again. See yourself stepping forward confidently now, just as you did then.

Now that you feel inspired and passionate about your project, it is time to start. Set your goal, determine the steps needed to achieve it and start - step by step - there is only yourself standing in your own way - so MOVE! Put those old, self-limiting beliefs in the bin and move forward now! Quick question for you: What happens if the first attempt does not succeed as hoped? Yes, of course. You try again! You examine the plan, look at the steps you took and examine what may have been missing or overlooked. Can this be seen from another angle? Try a different tack. Try anything - just promise me that you won't give up at the first hurdle. You deserve the success – sometimes you just have to try a few different things to get there. It is not a failure if it teaches you something. Try exercise 8.

2 WHEN MAKING A DECISION IS DIFFICULT

When making a decision is difficult, two parts of you are in conflict   When you feel torn and unable to decide you may say to yourself something like "a part of me wants to go out and socialise but another part of me just wants to stay in and chill". You have two different desires. Two different options. Opposing and equal. Two parts of your inner consciousness are conflicted as to what path is best for you.

Our subconscious mind has several parts working for us at all times. Their aim is to protect us and serve us. Each part takes on roles to keep us safe in whatever way it deems best. Sometimes those parts end up in direct conflict with opposing ideas on how to achieve the same result. In the example I gave here both parts want me to be happy – one through socializing and one through resting quietly at home, alone. Clearly, both ideas would be helpful, but I would have to choose between them.   The example here is a simple dilemma but life often presents us with far more complex and confusing problems.

Internal Family Systems by Dick Schwartz M.D. [1]explains how the parts in our minds work for us and details how best to engage with them so that the Self remains in control rather than lead by the parts which do not always *know* best, despite trying their best to protect us. One example of this would be when a person develops an addiction – to drugs, alcohol or gambling etc. The addiction is a way to protect that person from feeling the pain he or she is carrying within them. It is an effective way to numb or block the pain in the short term but obviously, it is not a wise strategy in the long term as addiction causes more pain on top of the existing pain the person is trying to escape.

Bearing in mind that our parts love us and are trying to protect us we must listen to both arguments and be grateful that they are so determined to keep us safe. We need to turn inwards and reflect upon the messages. We need to learn from what they are trying to teach us. Both parts will be protecting you and guiding you towards what it feels is best for you. Maybe one or the other is correct or maybe both. The Self – the You that needs to lead – will step forward in quiet times of reflection or meditation. Allow your Self to listen, understand and lead. Both parts need to recognise each other's validity and aim to love you. They need to compromise or collaborate. Your Self will lead the collaboration and allow the right decision to come from within.

---

[1] Internal Family Systems by Dick Schwartz M.D

Decisions bring consequences and it may be that fear steps in to block you. This fearful part wants to protect you from making mistakes, perhaps. In a way, if you do not act, you will not be able to make a mistake. The part succeeds in protecting you. However, it is clear that inaction means stagnancy. Being stuck. Frozen in fear. Procrastination is fear in disguise. The fearful part has hindered you unintentionally. It has held you back from making a decision and moving forward with your life. It has limited you.

Sometimes not making any decision *is* making a decision. Inaction is a decision. The outcome will follow from the lack of movement. Fear holds many people back in decision-making. Fear of making a mistake. Fear of the outcomes, especially if there is doubt as to how things will pan out. It is possible however, to become so frozen in inaction that life passes you by. There is an expression to nudge us on our path – "Feel the fear and do it anyway!" Or even, "Fear Everything And Run" which I replace with: "Face Everything And Rise".

Which adage would you choose to live by?

I would rather regret (regret is a strong word which I will come back to) having done something that did not work out, than regret not ever having tried. It is better to learn from mistakes than to not learn anything through fear-based inaction.

Choose your path – either way is better.

Try exercise 4 to see if it will encourage you to make a decision. If the two options do not feel right, maybe there's a third option waiting to be discovered. Open your heart and your eyes to new possibilities.

(Regret indicates sadness for me but for others it can be guilt and shame. Having made plenty of "mistakes" in the past (and I am sure, there are a good few still to come in my life as I continue to learn!) I refuse to guilt or shame myself. I made decisions and acted then with the information, knowledge and awareness that I had at that time in my life. As my awareness grew, I learned and was capable of making better choices later in life. However, some choices happen when they happen. They cannot be delayed indefinitely and so, we act with the awareness, resources and understanding that we have at that moment. We cannot regret this later as hindsight does not heal. It may enlighten us, but it cannot hold us in shame indefinitely.)

Let your Self step forward. Reflect quietly and calmly. Listen to your instincts, your heart, not your fear. What do you want? What do you need? How can this be achieved?

Try exercise 4, (as below) a technique from Neuro-Linguistic Programming[2] which will enable you to feel or intuit a decision. When overthinking or fear steps in, allow the Self to lead. This NLP exercise can allow you to feel the right outcome for you and allow you to make an informed decision.

---

[2] 2 Neuro-Linguistic Programming, Richard Bandler.

To choose between two paths –Travel down one path (physically walking) until you reach the point of 1 year or 5 years after having made Decision A. Turn around and look back at where you came from. How do you feel having reached this point in your life? Does it fill you with joy? Peace, satisfaction? Dread, unease? Excited? Relieved? Peaceful? Anxious? Disappointed?

Return to your starting point and walk down the second path until you reach 1 year or 5 years after Decision B. Turn around and look back at where you came from. How do you feel having reached this point in your life? Does it fill you with joy? Peace, satisfaction? Dread, unease? Excited? Relieved? Peaceful? Anxious? Disappointed?

Return to your starting point in present day and compare the feelings and emotions you experienced on both journeys. It may be very clear that one decision left you feeling much more positive than the other. Occasionally, neither pathway is clearly the "one" so perhaps it is back to square one and search again for alternative options, although this time-line pathway travel does generally leave you with a clear intuitive feeling of what to do next.

Allow inner conflict to fall aside with quiet reflection or meditation as an alternative to the time-line or in addition to it. Most important is that you remove fear from your path and allow the Self to lead. Either way is better than nowhere.

3 SUNFLOWERS TURN TOWARDS THE SUN

Are you currently feeling fulfilled in all aspects of your life? Take stock of where you are, who is in your life and what your purpose is. Do you spend quality time with the people who bring you peace and joy or with those who bring you toxic energy? Does your job give you great satisfaction or do you yearn for more? Are you in control of your daily life? Does your work fulfil you? What would you rather do? Is your home life a safe, loving environment in which to grow with support and acceptance?

I ask so many questions – please don't let them lead you into a spiral of despair! Asking with a curious and open heart will give you the chance to examine your life calmly and honestly. It will grant you the possibility to make changes where you realise they are needed in order to grow and raise your vibration.

Try exercise 2, The Wheel of Life, to assess which areas of your life merit your attention first. Which areas leave you feeling happy and fulfilled and which areas bring you disappointment or heartache? Reflect on each of the sections in your wheel – name them as you see fit but feel free to use the guide given as these are generally the areas in which life impacts us most. Family / relationships / friendships / career / money / health / personal growth etc. Take a moment in a quiet space and allow yourself to reflect upon how you "feel" about each area of your life, one by one. Do not over analyse or think – just feel.

Choose an area to focus on and you will grow towards aligning yourself to your true identity and happiness. Look at your current position - are you satisfied? are your needs being met? Did you know that sunflower is "tournesol" in French and "girasol" in Spanish. They both translate to "Turn to the sun", which describes exactly how the flower behaves. It knows instinctively to turn away from the dark shadows and into the light. We grow in the light of loving environments. We do not blame the flower for not growing but the environment in which it exists. The soil, sun/water ratio affect its growth. Why, then, should we expect humans to grow emotionally, mentally, spiritually in dark, toxic environments lacking in love and nurture. Turn to the sun, turn away from the negative and find your soul shines and your stature grows. Know your worth, feel it. Demand it. Actively seek it out just as the sunflower seeks the sun in order to grow tall.

4 HOW DO YOU MANAGE CONFLICT?

What happens when you are in conflict with someone? Are you able to view things from their perspective? Or, are you stubbornly steadfast that your opinion is the only one that counts?

It is vital that we can view situations from another person's perspective. Being able to consider how an outsider may view the situation broadens our own understanding and enlightens us. Look from another angle to find understanding and resolution. There are always different sides to a story. Yours, theirs, that of a third party looking in, society's view and perhaps even that of a spiritual belief system. Whose point of view is correct? Can something be learned by examining a situation from different perspectives?

When we remain stuck in own heads, believing that we know the correct course of action and that others are inferior or incapable, we lower our vibration. It may be that we do indeed have the answer and that the other people do not. Yet this does not diminish their input. When we look at a floorplan of a house, it gives us clear indication of the layout and space within. However, we cannot tell if the house is attractive or with what materials it has been constructed. When we look at the front aspect of the house, we can appreciate its attractiveness as a building yet have no true idea of its interior size or contents. Each point of view has its value. Putting all the views together, we can obtain a fuller picture, a deeper understanding. By listening to others, we add to our own knowledge.

Curiosity and compassion are important values to keep close in our lives. Being open to new ideas and points of view, being open-minded and open-hearted allows us to grow and become more enlightened. As I write this, I chastise myself for moments in my life when I have acted as though I knew it all and did not require input from others. This superiority is not an attractive quality. It is low vibrational and I let it go now. I aim to remain open and curious. It is good to be knowledgeable and to always strive to learn and be enlightened in new ways. I will continue on this path yet be mindful to remember that as I learn it shows that I still do not know everything. I will never know everything, for the world is huge, the universe is vast. I am but a part of it. I am but one voice, one mind and there are so many other voices to listen to and from which to learn. If I listen only to my own voice, I hear only what I already know – I learn nothing new.

Conflict with others is inevitable in life because we are all beautifully individual with our own opinions and beliefs and values. We will not all agree on everything and nor do we need to. It is our decision how to manage conflict, however.

If you experienced a traumatic childhood, you may be conflict avoidant in flight state. Leaving any situation the moment you sense tension or conflict arising. You may fight – refusing to let your guard down and acknowledge the validity of another's views. Stubbornly sticking to your opinion and arguing your justifications, unable to accept anybody's opinion. Fawn state is a third possible response – accepting and appeasing the other person, through merely agreeing and not voicing your own opinion. If you freeze you may find yourself voiceless again. Unable to establish boundaries for fear of upsetting the person further. Inaction being the response triggered. How do you personally respond to a conflict situation? How would you prefer to manage it?

Again, I call for curiosity and compassion – for all parties involved. Being open-hearted, open-minded and calm. Look for differences as well as commonalities. Appreciate the alternative views and allow the information to give you a bigger, fuller picture. See the whole house before deciding on your preferred view.

Try exercise 9 using Neuro-Linguistic Programming's Perceptual Positions[3] to open our minds and hearts to alternatives points of view. Stand and consider the problem /situation which concerns you from your point of view – state aloud in the *first* person how you feel about it. "*I* think…, *I* feel… *I* see … *I* want… / don't want … etc.)

---

[3] Neuro-Linguistic Programming, Richard Bandler and John Grinder

First position – your own personal point of view

Second position – the other person's point of view

Third position – an outsider's neutral point of view

You can continue to explore further if you choose with

Fourth position – the community's point of view (Business / society / club)

Fifth position – a spiritual point of view (whichever faith you choose)

5 FEAR IS MERELY A THOUGHT AND THOUGHTS CAN BE CHANGED

Fear is a powerful emotion created by thoughts, memories or trauma. It is imperative to remember that it is not a real thing that can hurt you. Fear is a self-protection tool that can sometimes misfire - an alarm that is too sensitive and goes off unnecessarily. Human beings are hard-wired to look out for danger – a saber-toothed tiger, a bear or any perceived threat to life in our ancient community. However, although our brains are hard-wired to look for danger or negativity, we can choose how much attention we pay it – do we want to focus on the negative and the danger? Or, face life with a positive outlook and optimism in our hearts. Our internal alarm system needs resetting.

The house alarm detects every mosquito that lands on the window at 2am. It senses the slightest breeze or the cat rubbing itself against the front door. The alarm screeches. It is far too sensitive to be effective. Reset the level of sensitivity and the alarm will keep you alerted to only real threats such as the burglar breaking in.

By resetting our own internal alarm – our parameters of fear and we will be alerted to only true dangers as it should be, keeping us safe crossing the road or while cooking with fire. Hyper-alertness created from trauma does not protect you but drains your energy and stops you from taking any kind of step forward. Fear may present itself as procrastination and failure to make decisions as we have seen. The longer we allow fear to dominate our decision making the harder it will be to free ourselves. Hypnotherapy can help break this life pattern. Fear has no power over me for fear is a thought and thoughts can be changed.

Phobias are an example of when fear goes too far. It is possible, through Neuro-Linguistic Programming and hypnotherapy, to reframe fear. Reframe it, and free yourself. Phobias generally develop from a traumatic moment that we experience at a young age or from seeing a parent scared by something which we then also learn to fear. Phobias can also be hereditary from grandparents or beyond, transmitted genetically. These phobias are best resolved through hypnotherapy. For a general non-hereditary phobia we can use Neuro-Linguistic Programming to reframe that original film or soundtrack of the initial sensitizing event that you are replaying in your mind and freeze it! Mute it! It is your movie, your creation, your thoughts. Take back control. Take its power away – step by step - drain its colour to make it insignificant and then blur it until it is a pointless shrinking inconsequential dot. You can no longer see it, hear it or feel it. It has no relevance in your life. Say goodbye to unnecessary fear. Try this exercise as explained in exercise 5.

6 I CAN GROUND MYSELF AND RELIEVE PANIC

Panic is a different kind of fear. It is a sign of your over-sensitive alarm – hyper-alertness being triggered. How do we manage moments of panic? Human beings have two types of fear hard-wired into our brains: Fear of falling and fear of loud noises. Both of which hark back to our primitive heritage – where we needed to be vigilant to protect ourselves and our communities. It is almost impossible to not jump when we hear a loud bang. We wake ourselves up from a dream where we are falling and we always wake before we land. Is panic connected to these hard-wired fears? Not necessarily, although loud noises such as shouting would trigger panic in some people such as those raised in homes where domestic abuse took place. Childhoods ruined by parents shouting, arguing or threatening create adults who suffer panic in later life as those somatic fears are awakened by the loud noise or shouting.

Panic comes from a deep-rooted sense of not being safe. Whether it comes from childhood trauma, a nightmare or a real-life situation, panic creates a strong physical response. Clients have described panic as a sharp stab in the chest, a tightening around the chest or racing pulse, hot flush and breaking out in sweat. All typical symptoms of panic. How does it affect you? When panic is something that happens to you occasionally then it is purely a natural physical response. However, if panic affects your daily life then it is time to reframe that panic and find a way to stay calm and rooted in reality. You are here, today in this moment, in this place. You are NOT back in the childhood home or at risk from past traumas. The somatic response is wired in due to repetitive occurrences but this can be undone. Neuroplasticity means that we can re-wire the messages your brain receives and transmits until you no longer respond in the old way and you are able to react in an alternative way which is more appropriate and acceptable. As your repeated response kicks in you can STOP it and tell yourself "I am safe" "This is now, this is today, this is here, I am safe"". With each occurrence where you can STOP the old response and REFRAME it - "I am safe" your brain will create a new neural pathway until you begin to respond automatically in the new calmer and more appropriate manner leaving the old ways behind now.

Learn to undo those old symptoms by reassuring yourself of how safe you are - in your calm, slow-breathing state, ground yourself by stating what you can see, what sounds you can hear, what can you smell. If the place you are in is not reassuring enough you can choose to recapture the positive emotions that a happy place creates for you. A safe place where you feel secure, cared for or happy. Imagine that place, see yourself there – name 5 things you can see there, 4 things you can touch, 3 things that you can hear, 2 things that you can smell and maybe 1 thing that you can taste - let those calming, pleasant emotions replace the anxiety that tried to derail you. Those thoughts and emotions are yours to control - close your eyes and do it now. Where is your safe, happy place? Imagine yourself there whenever you feel panic or anxiety. Stop the old responses and rewire the new.

7 I LET GO OF SELF-LIMITING BELIEFS

Who told you that you were not good at drawing? An art teacher who was stressed and in a bad mood that day? Who told you that you couldn't sing? A jealous friend? Who made you believe that you lacked ability, intelligence, were not beautiful or loveable? To be blunt, it was not you who created these self-limiting beliefs, but it IS you that is choosing to continue to carry them with you now. Let the Autumn trees teach you how beautiful it is to let things go. These thoughts grew within you but now it is time to let them fall away.

Stop for a moment and examine each negative thought that you carry. Each thought that limits you and holds you back. What are you hearing? Whose voice are you believing? Turn that thought around and imagine what could happen for you.

Stop letting self-limiting beliefs hold you back! They do not define you! Stop with the negative self-talk. Stop blocking your exciting future by holding onto outdated and inaccurate ideas! Start looking at yourself with fresh eyes – see your potential. See yourself achieving your goals – visualise your success. Who or what is stopping you? Don't let it be YOU!

What would happen for you if you realised that you are capable? What would happen for you if you realised that you are loveable? That you are intelligent? That you are creative? That you are talented? That you are attractive? Now, which belief would you rather carry with you? Write down your answers to the following questions keeping in mind a specific self-limiting belief.

What would happen if you tried to achieve a specific goal?

What would happen if you didn't try?

What would *not* happen if you tried?

What would *not* happen if you *didn't* try?

Who wins with these self-limiting beliefs? Not you, certainly. Your life remains limited and hampered. *I* know that you deserve to live a life unlimited and free. It's *your* turn to believe this too.

Your mindset is powerful but it is *you* who controls it. Do you choose to have a positive or a negative mindset. Do you want to see life with optimism or with dread? Would you prefer to look for the good in people or always expect the worst of human nature? It is not easy to switch from negative to positive. It is a daily challenge to reprogram your mindset, but it can be done. With repeated actions, habits form. One cigarette is just one cigarette but after smoking thirty cigarettes it will become a habit. Writing positive statements and notes of gratitude for one week will raise your spirits but if you choose to do this every day for 30 days a beautiful habit will form. Should you continue to complete these same thoughts and actions for 90 days it becomes a lifestyle. The neuroplasticity of the human brain means it is never too late to change one's habits and create new ones. It is this beautiful ability of the human brain that hypnotherapists and wellbeing coaches love. Your brain can be retrained to stop the old, automatic behaviours that have become undesirable and unpleasant. They hold you back and block your progress. Your awareness has brought you to an understanding of what your obstacles are and you now seek a way to overcome them. Your brain repeatedly stops the old unwanted thoughts and creates a new neural pathway to a new preferred life choice. Hypnotherapy can help plant the seed, but you must want to make the change for you need to implement it each time until it does indeed, become the automatic new behaviour.

Each time you allow a negative self-belief to control your outcome you blindly repeat the same negative thoughts and actions or non-actions, staying stuck in procrastination or fear. Stop! Challenge that thought, look at where it may have begun. Does it still remain true? Are you still worthless? Who says so? Can you not sing?

When a limiting belief pops into your head and tries to stop you from trying something I want you to shout in your head "STOP!" Imagine a big red STOP road sign right in your face. Put your hand out palm away from you as you shout

"STOP!" That pathway is no longer accessible. It is no longer valid. You need an alternative. Initially it may not ring true with you that you can sing or that you are capable. So, what you replace the old belief with now must be plausible for your unconscious mind to accept. Change the negative thoughts to "I can try to sing and it will be a fun challenge" or "I am getting better each time I try this"; "Each time I try, I make progress"; "When I challenge myself, I feel good about myself". Once you repeat the new phrases and STOP the old automatic responses the new phrases will become the automatic thoughts and beliefs. Once you start to believe you can try you may find yourself believing you can succeed. Because you can.

8 NOTHING LASTS FOREVER

It is important to recognise when you have pushed through hard times and come out the other side. It is essential to accept that you will not always be on your best form, your highest self may not always shine and you may, indeed, experience negative feelings and thoughts. That's ok. You are human. It happens. But it's temporary. It will pass and it will start to feel easier again. Storms pass and sunshine dries the rain.

Well done on not giving up, for digging in and keeping on going. Well done for recognizing your needs – knowing when to rest and step back completely. Pause. Breathe. Restart. It may not have been a conscious decision and you may well have resorted to your trauma response of flight, fight, freeze or fawn in order to survive this situation. Initially, we act automatically but over time and with growing awareness we can begin to manage emotionally charged situations with greater consciousness and calmness. Once our heightened emotions controlled us but soon, we learned to control our emotions.

Sometimes the mountain seems enormous but if you focus on the first step in front of you and don't look too far ahead at the clouds you will save yourself from becoming overwhelmed. When life is hard and dark remember to care for yourself – find rest, space, have patience and compassion for yourself. It will pass. Nothing lasts forever. The sun reappears after the moon as day follows night.

Life never stays still, so, just as the bad times pass so do the good times. The great highs that we seek and enjoy are transient also. We must remember that as life passes each day brings either negative or positive things and we must be strong to endure and open to enjoy. Be grateful and open in order to fully enjoy the good times. Stay in the happy moments as long as you can and recall them in the darker days. It will pass. Nothing lasts forever, which may seem negative but I see it more as a reminder and encouragement. It tells me that in my dark moments I will recover, life will improve – nothing is eternal and I will find my sunshine again. The wonderful happy times will also pass by, not lasting endlessly. They last longer than the sad days, that is for sure – because that is also my choice. I do not wish to sit in the dark – I take steps to raise my vibration, shift my mindset and lighten my day. In the happy times, I try to stay open and grateful and aware fully of how special these moments are – never taken for granted, but appreciated and treasured. It is natural for life to move between highs and lows and the variety is the colour within our lives. Learning to be mindful of our past traumas and working through pain with a counsellor or hypnotherapist will allow us to enjoy the ride as the highs are not too high and the lows, not too low. The extremes some people have experienced no longer have the power to control their lives and leave them mentally and emotionally shattered. We do not want to just survive life; we want to thrive. When life feels as though it is something to be endured, or survived, take steps to seek help from a qualified therapist because you deserve better.

REFRESH

1 WHEN YOU KNOW BETTER, DO BETTER

Have compassion and forgiveness - for yourself. Human beings are not robots. We are not machines. We are fallible and that is part of our charm! Some mistakes are small and insignificant but some can be bigger with more serious consequences. There is not a single person in this world who has not made a mistake. It is time to reassess how you have judged yourself and criticised yourself for your errors.

Whatever you recriminate yourself for cannot be changed now. It is done. The consequences have played out. The past is the past, and we move on and we learn. Hopefully; If we have sufficient self-awareness.

Be kind to yourself for past mistakes - you did the best you could with the knowledge, understanding and awareness that you had at the time. Now that you *know* better you can *do* better.[4] So look with kindness on your past self - forgive your mistakes, learn and move forward. Emotional maturity

---

[4] Maya Angelou

comes with age – but, at times, even age does not bring wisdom. Society and especially the surroundings and adults, such as parents, carers or teachers, that we have in our early years form our beliefs, attitudes and behaviours. Unfortunately, they do not necessarily teach us the wisest ways to live and view the world. We must understand that even they, as adults, may not have known better. They may have had their own traumas to survive. They may not have had the emotional maturity and sense to teach us better. They, too, may have had parents who failed them.

We often find the generational curse of mistreating children and the damage thereby caused, continues until somebody, somewhere in the family decides to stop it. If you were criticised and belittled, neglected and shown no love or affection you grew up unsafe, emotionally and perhaps physically too. This impacts strongly in the child growing up. Often, although not always, the child recreates the same dynamic in their family and again the cycle continues. I write this in order to explain, not blame. Until we educate ourselves and determine if what we have learned early on truly aligns with ourselves as we grow in life, we have only our own childhoods as a reference. We can only act according to the knowledge we have. Fortunately, people are seeing that these repeated patterns are unhealthy and undesirable. They want better. They deserve better and so do their children. So be compassionate and loving towards yourself and past mistakes. If you are showing up each day, trying to be better and do better now, accept that the past is the past and it is a lesson learned. For now that we know better we can choose to do better. The failure here would be to not change your behaviour despite the newly acquired knowledge, for that would no longer be a mistake but rather a conscious decision to behave in that way. That would be ignorant and that would be unforgiveable.

2 HOW DO YOU VIEW YOURSELF?

Look again and see that you have always been enough.[5]

It is easy to believe negative comments made about us and far harder to accept the compliments we receive. The negative always wins over the positive seeing that this hypervigilance for danger is hard-wired into our primitive brains. It takes seven compliments to undo the damage of one insult. It is modern day society which teaches us to be so self-critical, to compare ourselves, mostly unfavourably, with others. In this age of social media and hi-tech we are taught that external beauty is so important. More important than the soul, thoughts and actions of the person. We are presented with filtered and fake images of perfection. Flawless faces and bodies which belie reality and convince us even more that we are just not good enough. How can we compare with the images we are fed?

---

[5] Marisa Peer, *I am enough*

I am so grateful that growing up in the seventies and eighties I never had a mobile phone or social media to contend with. My mistakes are firmly unrecorded or available for scrutiny by all. My bullying took place in school and stayed there, thankfully. I was insecure enough to have eating disorders even without the pressures teenagers have to endure these days. We had magazines and of course, back then, we had no idea that photographs were altered or enhanced. Yet, even knowing what we do nowadays we still allow feelings of inferiority and insecurity to control our thoughts.

We learn, unjustly, that we are not good enough, not pretty enough, not thin enough, not clever enough, just not enough! Who says so?! Who gets to decide who is enough? We are born into this world with nothing but our bodies and souls. This was all we needed. We were perfect. Just as God, the universe, or whoever you believe in, designed us to be. We are always enough - we have always been enough.

It is time that we unlearn the damaging mindset of imperfection and inferiority. We need to learn to accept ourselves for who we are, for how we look, for how we speak, for how we are, each of us, individual and unique. There is nobody better than me. There is no person worse than me. We are all human beings and perfect as we are. Of course, the behaviours and beliefs we have gathered since our births may have tarnished our perfection along the way but the beauty is that we are capable of learning and retraining our brains, of improving ourselves, spiritually, educationally, emotionally, in all senses. Nothing has to remain the same, if we choose to work on ourselves, and I believe you do, as you chose to read this book, we can grow into beautiful souls who are enlightened, self-aware and positive examples for the world.

I am wise enough to know that me simply writing here that you are perfect is not going to change your point of view instantly. Your thoughts will need to change over time. You will need to grow to believe in the new truths. You will have to rid your brain of the negative mindset, which instantly puts you in the shade. One way is through neuroplasticity – rewiring your brain by repeating positive affirmations over the course of 30 days, 90 days and beyond if necessary. Remember that positive statements such as "I am perfect" will probably be rejected by your unconscious mind, as it is not true. It's a lovely thought, but not true. Therefore, it is vital that you phrase the affirmation in such a way as to make it believable and agreeable as well as a morale and ego boost.

Try positive affirmations such as "I am enough", I love myself as I am", "I am unique, I am special, I am me." "I am working on becoming a better me", "I am working towards my ideal body"; Look in the mirror and smile at the beautiful soul evolving.

3 ARE YOU LOOKING AT YOURSELF THROUGH OTHER PEOPLE'S EYES?

Do you hear yourself saying "should"? "I should do this" or "I should be further in my career!" "I should be married by now" or "I should not be behaving like that"? Stop and reflect a moment what you are saying to yourself and why.

What does "should" mean? It is a word which implies necessity or obligation. It is a modal verb such as words like "must", and "have to". There is a sense of obligation and burden. It does not imply positivity, rather more a critical or negative point of view. When you say "should" in your head do you hear a parent's voice making you doubt yourself or criticising you? Do you hear your unhappy partner's voice? Do you hear your boss or colleagues mocking you? How much power do you allow these people, these voices to have over you?

Do you allow the opinions of others to diminish your own? How often do we start to doubt ourselves in favour of the more confident or domineering voice? It is not unusual to be almost brainwashed or dominated by a figure of authority, whose opinions are thrust upon us so confidently and frequently. We gather rules of society and norms of behaviour from our early caregivers. We form beliefs and learn behaviours early in life so how we behave is led by our parents, carers, teachers. We get to choose later in life if we still feel those learned behaviours fit our mindset or serve us in reality. Occasionally, we realise that the ways of our parents are not *our* ways. This could refer to silly, insignificant things such as the football team we support, to major issues such as how to discipline our children.

Do you live your life freely or constrained by the views and beliefs of other people? Do you live life freely choosing according to your instincts and knowledge or limited by other people's opinions and demands? Whilst it is good to learn from others and take guidance on social etiquette and morality, we are still free individuals to choose the way we live our life. We can acknowledge people's experience and wisdom and be grateful for their suggestions – when you ask for them, but when uninvited advice hinders your progress and confuses your mind, you may need to set a boundary and limit that person's access to your headspace. I can admire my elders' experience and what they have learned through their lives and still be aware that my experience in my generation does not necessarily align with theirs. I can admire and respect their views but they, in return, must respect my views and ultimately, my decision. After all, this is my life.

We are free to choose the career or partner or lifestyle we want. We are free to turn away from behaviours, people and environments which do not feel right for us. We get a choice – just as your parents or teachers did. There is more than one way to do everything in this universe. There is more than one point of view. There are many perspectives to any situation. Either way is better. No one person is correct in every situation. Why, then do we feel the weight of their opinion when we are faced with choice?

Try exercise 5 to rid negative self-talk. Take the outspoken, uninvited voice out of your head and into your thumb nail. Hold it in front of you, arm outstretched. Let the voice speak to you from your thumbnail. Let its voice be Mickey Mouse or amusing in any way. Let it sound so ridiculous that you could never take it seriously. How can something so silly have any power over you?

We only have one life to live - so live it *your* way. You get to choose – you get to make mistakes. You get to learn from them. You get to do things nobody would ever imagine you were capable of. It is your decision. How exciting!

4 CHOOSE TO BE A SURVIVOR NOT A VICTIM

Being a victim means that you have no control over what happens to you. This may have been the case in a traumatic situation - but one you have survived. Trauma takes many forms; it causes much damage and hurt but it does not need to define who you are or what you achieve. You did not invite or cause hurt to be done to you, or to cause what you may have witnessed. You did not cause someone to hurt you or others. You are not to blame. In your innocence, you are a victim of another's actions. You have survived this, for you are still here, physically. You may bear scars, physically and/or emotionally but you are still living. You are a survivor. Are you just surviving though? Are you living? There is a big difference between surviving day by day, clinging on by your fingernails, white-knuckling it from morning to night and living life, really, fully *living*. Embracing new opportunities, letting go of the past, feeling free to achieve and become who want to become.

Your response, your fight against the psychological hurt, sets you apart - victim or survivor. Do you choose to sit in negative energy, helpless and self-pitying or do you choose to allow self-awareness and healing to happen - work through the pain and understand the situation and yourself better. Self-acceptance and a recognition of your pain and how it has affected you thus far will allow you to break free. Its grip holding you back is weakened and you will be able to set yourself free to move forward now. It takes courage and support but survivors can and do take back their control.

What is self-acceptance? How does this help me to heal from abuse or trauma? When you think about yourself, do you speak kindly about yourself? Do you notice the good qualities you have, the strength and courage, the resilience and optimism? Do you only see the negative traits? Your "failings"? Do you blame yourself for what happened to you? Do you still feel that you deserved it? That it happened to you because you caused it? Because you were not loveable? Because you were not worthy? Stop these dark thoughts as they are confused and the thoughts of a wounded child who tried to rationalise what happened to them. None of this was that child's fault. The child did not invite or cause the abuse. This was purely the act of a damaged person who does not know how to love correctly, does not know how to heal their own wounds; someone lost and sad; Understanding that the abuser was damaged and hurting begins to explain the situation. It does not excuse or pardon it. It does not negate the hurt it caused. It should serve to allow the child to remove the burden of guilt and shame from *their* shoulders. If your trauma is caused by abuse, please seek professional help to clear your negative emotions. You deserve to be free from shame, guilt or misunderstanding your worth. You are not a victim when you learn to free yourself from the pain. Take control of the narrative – take control of your life now. Do you want the past to dictate your future still? It happened to you; it did not define you. Do not allow it to limit you. Do not allow someone's failure to see your worth to diminish how you see yourself.

It is time to thrive – not just survive. With love and respect, I ask that you consider seeking professional help in order to fully live your life, freely and with joy.

5 I FOCUS MYSELF IN THIS MOMENT

What has been, is gone, what is to come is still unknown. Dwelling on the past is a potential path to depression and worrying about the future can lead you to anxiety. Being fully present in this moment, where you are, what you are doing, who you are in this moment - is everything - it is all there is. Breathe and recognise all that is around you at this time and live this fully with your whole attention and focus.

Time is a concept which many debate. Time travel, quantum leaps, alternate dimensions and more. The one certain in all debates about time is that there is no other time than the present. This moment exists. And then it doesn't. It has already passed and no longer exists. Tomorrow is never here for when it arrived it became today. So, the only true time that exists is NOW.

Staying in this moment, granting it your full attention is a gift to yourself. Make space for yourself and the opportunity to truly be present in the now. It is so rare that any of us actually stop and reflect. Life is always so busy and frantic.

We are overwhelmed with responsibilities, duties, worries and stresses. When do we actually just stop and *be*? Be present, be still, be calm, be quiet, be us. What we can learn by stopping and being is limitless peace and freedom. A moment (or longer if you can) of respite from the daily worries, the sadness or nostalgia of time gone by, from fears and anxieties of what is to come, or tasks you still need to do.

Take ten minutes each day for yourself. Even the busiest person can find ten minutes to remove themselves from "busy-ness". Find a quiet space if you can, even better if it can be outdoors in nature. Look around you and pay attention to details. Look at the trees, the leaves, the bark; are there any nests or activity in the trees? What can you hear? Are there birds? People? Quiet and stillness? Is the wind blowing? What temperature is the air? What can you smell? What can you touch? The grass? Your own hands? Fill your senses and appreciate fully what this moment brings you. If thoughts of jobs to do or other pressures, try to push into your mind put them in a cloud and watch them blow past you on the wind. Thoughts may come and you let them go; it will take practice to stop yourself from being pulled into each thought. The more you allow them to simply float in and out the easier it will become for you to relax and quieten your mind and stay focused on this very moment of now.

Thinking of the past brings memories and perhaps, regret, looking to the future brings uncertainty and doubts. Both actions can also be positive, do not misunderstand. Nostalgia can bring us happiness through remembering special moments and we can be excited and optimistic for special events coming up. I do not wish to take that from you. I hope just to allow you to free yourself from the unwanted and unnecessary pressures from past things which you cannot change and with which you must come to terms, and from future events for which you cannot predict nor fully prepare.

We all are working towards future goals, and it is essential that we learn from experience, yes, but we need to remember that we are neither held back by the hurt from the past nor are we blocked by fear of the future. Practice mindful living for 10 minutes each day. Being in the moment can be freeing and expansive and essential to our mental wellbeing.

6 I AM UNIQUE

I am unique and bring my own blend of skills, talents and personality. There is nobody like you. You are one of a kind. Nobody has quite the same combination of skills and abilities, strengths and weaknesses. Nobody has your sense of humour combined with your values and personal qualities. Each one of us is a unique blend. Each one of us will be loved and valued by someone special, or recognised as worthy by our friends or colleagues. Each one of us will have self-doubt at one point in our lives. What a shame that is. What a waste of energy. We are not perfect and we can allow that. We can choose to work towards improving the areas of our lives in which we feel we can grow and always remain open to constructive criticism with a compassionate and curious heart. Noticing where we can grow is not the same as seeing ourselves as failures. Living is dying.[6] Nothing remains the same and we can choose where to stay stuck or where to move forward.

---

[6] Dzongsar Khyentse Rinpoche

The first step forward is recognising our own uniqueness, our own beauty and our own strength.

Take a moment to reflect upon your strengths, your personality qualities. What do you admire about yourself? What are you proud of? List your top three characteristics (or as many as you can) and recognise how special you are – be unashamedly you. Be proud of you – you are amazing!

As difficult and uncomfortable as you may feel praising yourself repeat this task regularly in order to become more confident in yourself and more comfortable in seeing your worth. See how much easier it becomes with practice. Once you can see your own worth it will shine for others to see.

Do you believe that you need a degree to be valued? Do you believe that you need to be thin to be attractive? Do you believe that you need to speak with a certain accent in order to be considered intelligent? Do you minimise your value by creating strange limiting beliefs such as these?

Are you smart? Intelligence shows itself in many different forms. Common sense, academic achievement, entrepreneurial success, running a home within budget, caring for your family's needs, knowing the best way to serve your customers. How do you judge yourself – negatively or from a different perspective where you see that you do, indeed, have something to offer.

Are you beautiful? Who classifies what is and is not beautiful? Bear in mind that what one person finds ugly another finds beautiful. Where one person prefers slim-fit another may want more to cuddle. There is no one-size-fits-all. We are all beautiful whatever shape or size we may be. Love yourself for what you are; exercise and eat healthily to love and honour your body but remember to live life too.

Whoever told you that you were boring, not funny or dull merely projects their own self-doubt. There is someone in this world who finds you the most interesting, attractive person ever. Find those who see your style, your wisdom, your humour, your beauty. Find those who truly see your soul. Never settle for ignorant people who are blind to your sparkle. When you truly see your own worth you will never settle again. Open your eyes. Then open your heart.

7 YOU DESERVE TO BE HEARD, ACCEPTED AND LOVED FOR WHO YOU ARE

If you fail to see your own worth, you will always choose people who don't see it either. You set boundaries which tell others how to treat you. Subconsciously you send out signals so that others know whether they can give you the bare minimum effort, or if they need to treat you with respect. If you constantly put yourself last, always catering to others' needs first, people will take that as a sign that they can also put you last and not consider your needs. That is cruel and selfish but you are setting up this situation yourself.

When you take time to recognise what you need from others, from life – in career or in personal relationships, you will no longer tolerate disrespect. If you show others respect and kindness then surely, you too deserve the same? Why would you tolerate anything less? Only a person who feels that they are "less" would tolerate it. Less capable, less important, less loveable, less worthy. Who told you that you were less? Who made you believe that you were less important? What events in your life confirmed this self-limiting belief?

I have said this so many times and will continue to repeat it until everyone understands it completely. Nobody is better than you and nobody is worse than you. We are all different and unique and have our own wonderful combination of skills, talents and personality traits. Nobody should ever make you feel as though you are somehow less important than any other person. If somebody tried to do this, step forward. Their attempts to belittle you reveal their own insecurities. Projection is a telling sign that they fear rejection, abandonment or ridicule. They are not as secure and confident as they appear to be. It is sad. People who regularly criticise and shame others are hurting and do not know how to regulate their emotions or manage difficult situations in their own life. Understanding their behaviour may help you to accept that their words have less validity than you grant them. They are simply not true. Why would you unquestioningly accept their cruel words as truth? Yes, it is human nature to readily accept criticism rather than accept compliments but this is something we can change. With practice.

I have never met a perfect person or someone who has every aspect of their life wonderfully established and managed with no difficulties or failures. Each one of us has troubles and issues at some point in our lives. I must be very blessed as I seem to attract at least three major issues to contend with simultaneously rather than one at a time! I guess that's because I am an overachiever! Seriously though, life is never simple or straightforward. There will always be challenges. Some will be small whilst others may turn our worlds upside down. As we learn new skills and techniques to remain calm and look at things from different perspectives, and with the understanding that all things pass, good and bad, we will learn to manage these challenges more easily. Life is beautiful but can be dark; there may be periods of time which may be smooth and calm when suddenly things change dramatically. We have overcome trauma before, we can do it again. We harness past experience and resilience and calmly navigate our way through the current challenge. We may not be perfect but we are growing in strength and self-belief and we can survive, because we have before. Even when the moon is not whole, it still shines. We may struggle but we get through the phase and move onto a different phase, just as the moon does.

You deserve to be respected, to be heard, seen and appreciated for all that you are as well as all that you are not. You are a valued member of this universe, bringing your unique self to the lives of others. Love yourself, value yourself, whole or fragmented, you still matter and have worth. Let your true Self shine for all to see.

8 I AM LEARNING TO RECOGNISE MY EMOTIONS

I am learning to recognise my emotions and with compassion and acceptance, I can learn to manage them. Start each day with a moment of quiet reflection. Meditate and connect with your inner self. Allow your current feelings to communicate with you. Listen to the sensations in your body – any tension, any fast heartbeat or tightness in your chest. Any sore throat or stiff back – all somatic signals for stress or unease. Read the signs, sit with them and ask them to tell you what you need to understand.

Today I cried. I did not know why I was crying but it was a true sob. I allowed myself the release as my parasympathetic nervous system reset itself through crying. I reflected on my thoughts and what triggered the emotional response. I stumbled across a word that I had said to myself and as I said it again I cried again. It just jumped up through my chest into my throat, my shoulders hunched up, I lost my breath and my eyes wept. Loss. It was such a strong reaction I could not say the word aloud for a while. It kept choking me. My throat literally would not allow me to form the sound. I knew this was a breakthrough in understanding something important. To respond so dramatically to a word or phrase means that something you have kept repressed is fighting its way out, trying to be heard.

I sat with this strong emotional response and examined what emotion I was experiencing. Loss. I initially felt overwhelming sadness. Yet this did not fully describe what I was feeling. There was more to this sadness. I had to look beyond the initial layer to find more: Bereavement. Hurt. Pain. Anger. Injustice. I was surprised to find anger. I did not recognise my sadness as anger. It was as though a little girl was so sad but in reality, she was so angry at what had happened to her; to the injustice; to her powerlessness; to her invisibility; to not being heard; not being considered; not being valued; Being abandoned. Oh, that hurt.

It is powerful and almost overwhelming to examine your feelings and to allow them to truly communicate with you. It is your unconscious mind sharing with your conscious mind something that it needs to be aware of. Telling it to deal with something that it has been avoiding. The emotions break through as a sign that they need to be acknowledged. The pain cannot be ignored indefinitely. It will break through at times until you face it and deal with it. I have not dealt with all of my pain, it seems. There is more inner child work still to be done. I will meditate and allow the hurting child within to unburden her pain so that I can relieve it.

I need to show myself compassion and kindness. I am far too quick to criticise myself and tell myself off for not being further down the road on my healing journey. I hear myself saying "I should have dealt with that by now. How can this still be hurting me so much?" Why do I use "should" with myself when I ban it from my clients' vocabulary? I blame myself for things that were beyond my control, I criticise myself for not being more confident or trusting in myself. I hear myself as a therapist telling my clients that they cannot blame themselves for situations beyond their control. I know the truth of the situation and can help my clients but I have so far not heeded my own advice. Healer, heal thyself! I believe it is because of my pain, my traumas, my experiences, that I can understand and empathise so deeply with those that I help. Our situations may be different but I know pain. I want my clients to free themselves from their pain. I want to free myself from my pain. I deserve to love and care for my own inner child, my adult Self, and allow myself time and space to heal.

RENEW

1 WHAT NEEDS TO LEAVE YOUR LIFE IN ORDER TO MAKE SPACE FOR SOMETHING BETTER?

It is human nature to fear change. Change is unknown and scary. However, change also represents progress. Nothing can improve if it does not change. It is true that we can make changes that do not improve but rather impede growth at times. How will we know, though, if we do not try? Standing still, staying stuck with the status quo, doing the same thing over, and over will never bring a different result or forward motion.

We hold on to things, jobs, people, or relationships, too tightly, for too long sometimes, when really, by doing this, we are damaging ourselves. We would be more successful or more productive or fulfilled in a different job if we could face the fear of leaving the familiar and branching out. We may be happier if we could bring ourselves to leave a relationship that no longer works for us.

We may feel freer to learn and explore more about our true selves and our potential once we remove the toxic or negative things from our life.

Everything needs a space in our life. We need to invite happiness or success into our life – they don't just appear as if by magic. We need to make space for the new by removing the old. Imagine a runway blocked by a stationary plane - the incoming plane has nowhere to land – Once you let the old plane leave there is space to welcome in the new arrival. Your ideal job is waiting for you, your soul mate is desperate to find you but should those spaces already be taken and blocked they cannot find their way to you. Make space. Recognise what is *not* for you so that you can welcome what *is* for you. Remember, there is no moment too late – whatever is meant for you will never pass you by. It is up to you when it comes to you – when you make space and allow it to enter your life. I understand that it is painful to let go and difficult to escape certain situations but find a way out and you can open the door to new fresh and exciting possibilities. It is an age-old proverb that when one door closes another opens. So, look at your life with curiosity and compassion. What door do you need to close in order to welcome in your new opportunities for happiness?

The prettiest eyes have cried the most tears and the kindest hearts have felt the most pain. It is in feeling joy and pain and the beauty and agony of authentic emotion that we grow and learn. One of the hardest things to do is to let go of disappointment; to grieve the future that never happened and never will; to experience the loss of dreams, hopes and expectations that were never fulfilled. It hurts because although it was never a concrete reality it was your hope, and as it never realised it *is* a loss. Loss is an empty black hole and it hurts. This word strikes me hard in my chest. I know the pain of loss far too well. I am still working on managing my pain because I am still a work in progress, as we all are. I am learning to "let it go" Let go of the dreams and accept reality. Sit with the pain, understand how I am affected by the loss. Show myself patience and compassion whilst I am grieving and not hurry myself. Healing takes time and that is ok. I realise that I pressure myself to be all healed and ready for anything and then I am surprised when something triggers me. I need to heed my own advice. Allow myself space to grieve, to reflect and to let my emotions be. Understanding that the loss was because it was not my path allows me to come to a quiet acquiescence. I accept that although painful, there is a lesson for me to learn and grow from. Allow that message to come through to you in the quiet moments of reflection. The pain subsides and clarity helps you to move forward. Learn when to walk away – from a relationship, a job, a home – whatever it may be. Make space for something better. It is waiting for you.

2 I CHOOSE TO MOVE FORWARDS EACH DAY WITH COURAGE AND HOPE

Start your day with a conscious decision about how you want to live this day. Take a moment to check in with yourself. What intentions do you have, what goals do you have for today? What fears are trying to stop you? How does your body feel? What is it trying to communicate to you? Some days life is overwhelming, and other days it is manageable. What steps can you take to make each day better? Recognise and appreciate where you are and how you are succeeding, even if only in simple ways, like getting up and dressed. For some people getting dressed or washed is a great achievement on some days. For others they have no hesitation to charge into million-pound business deals. Who is to say which is braver? Courage is what it is for each person. Do not waste energy comparing yourself to another. By all means allow yourself to be inspired and motivated by others but do not allow negative comparisons to dampen your spirit. Look within yourself and decide what you want to achieve each day - a goal - small or big - be brave and take a step towards it. Even a small step is forward movement.

Courage is found within us as we step forward to attempt any task. Putting ourselves out there to speak to a stranger, a boss, a romantic possibility – all little risks require a level of courage. We can all find courage to some degree because we have all taken a risk at some point in our lives even if we do not think so. You went to school or nursery school – you engaged with the other children and the staff there. You may not even recall these interactions but you navigated your way through a big moment. There have been plenty of moments when you have needed to take a leap of faith, be brave and try something new or different, pushing yourself beyond your comfort zone. Well, that is where growth happens – outside your comfort zone. Staying stuck inside the familiar safety net you have created for yourself is your own cage, your own obstacle to escape. You may stay safe and cosy, risking little but also receiving little. If you repeat the same thing do not expect a different outcome. Rewards are for the brave.

When we can be brave, even in a small way, we win. We know we can do it, we can achieve something. Each day set a goal, each day expand it. Allow yourself to hope. Hope for more, achieve more, receive more. Hope is the light that encourages us forward. Start each day with the hope lighting your morning as you consider your day and set forward courageously.

Do not allow fear to hold you back - a little hope and courage each day as you set your intentions for the day ahead will set you on a positive, forward moving track. Each day a step further and after one year you are 365 steps further along your winning path.

3 THE MOMENT YOU RECOGNISE LIFE AS A BLESSING IT BECOMES ONE

Life drifts by, day by day and we can sometimes, allow it to *happen* to us, not paying attention to any of it. We get stuck in passivity and boredom. We don't take any risks, we don't challenge ourselves, we don't fully embrace life. We don't open our eyes and see what we have. This is surviving, merely existing with no active participation on our part. Why do we allow life to simply happen to us as though we have little to no influence over our lives?

We sit in a state of victimhood where we take no responsibility for our situation. It is very easy to live life in victimhood. Bemoaning our fate. Whining about the misfortunes that have befallen us. Well, life *is* tough. It is difficult and we all face challenges at some point in our lives. I do not belittle or negate trauma and serious issues, of course not. I have had my fair share of those too. However, if we stayed staring at our hurts and our suffering, we would never be able to pick ourselves up, face the future with optimism and courage. I refuse to sit still and not push forward. There is far more life and more exciting things to *do* with my remaining life, than what has happened to me in the past. I remain excited and hopeful because what I have realised is that happiness is a mindset. Positivity is a choice. I can choose to be happy, grateful and optimistic or I can allow pessimism and darkness to govern my thoughts. Once you can open your eyes and see that your life is a blessing, it truly starts to feel like one. It is YOUR choice though. It is your decision to change your perspective on your life. View things through a different lens and you may start to feel more optimistic about challenges, you may feel more courageous about taking risks.

When once I would wake with dread and a foggy mind, lacking enthusiasm and motivation, now I wake, grateful for the sleep I have had (even if it was broken sleep, I recognise the blessing of having had some rest). I start each day with gratitude. I wake grateful that I am comfortable in my warm bed, in my home, with my family, who are all safe. I am grateful for the new opportunity I have in this new day. Excited to discover new things, thoughts and experiences. Ready to learn and grow, even if sometimes the lessons hurt. I am grateful that I am blessed with the skills I have to accomplish whatever work I undertake – even if sometimes that work is difficult or unpleasant. I am fortunate that I am capable and educated sufficiently to do it. I am privileged and by seeing work from this point of view allows me to maintain my positivity and motivation and my ability to be my best self.

Take a moment to view your life from the eyes of another person. How fortunate do they see you? Are you homeless or do you have somewhere to stay safe at night? Are you unemployed or do you have a means to pay for yourself? Are you alone or do you have at least one good friend you can call upon? Are you physically and mentally healthy? There are so many ways in which you are blessed. There are so many things for which you can be grateful. It does not mean your life is perfect, or that your pain is not valid or recognised, but you are wise enough to see your blessings for what they are and to see which areas you need to work on in order to improve your life. (We do not compare our woes against those of another – it is not healthy to negate our sadness or troubles merely as they don't seem "as bad" or "as traumatic" as someone else's.) Spend some time each day thankful for the blessings you have and remain open to receiving more. Try exercise 10.

4 RIVERS FLOW AT THEIR OWN PACE

When others tell you that you should be married by 24, have children by 26 and have your life mapped out by whatever age they deem appropriate please close your ears. Whose life are they managing? Who is living YOUR life? We are all individuals and unique. We all have desires and fears, hopes, dreams and goals. Nobody knows our hearts as well as we do. Nor do they understand what we are experiencing on a daily basis. Some of us live life with fewer burdens or traumas than others, but we are all fighting our way to happiness.

We are not racing. We are not competing. We are living our lives, one day at a time. At our own pace. A flower does not think of competing with the flower next to it – it just blooms. In all its unique beauty. Brooks, streams, rivers, all flow at their own pace, navigating their own obstacles, dips and turns. Let yourself flow at your own pace without recrimination or self-doubt or criticism. You will know if you need to act if you are in need of a bump but it is your choice to nudge yourself forward. Listen to your heart not other people's timelines.

Here I am in this day, in this place. I am living and aware of my circumstances. I can be grateful or I can be critical. It is my choice. Regardless of my attitude, there can be no doubt that I am where I am. Through my action or inaction. Through circumstances that have befallen me, or that I have brought about. The position I am currently in may be positive, negative or blandly adequate. However, I am right where I need to be in this moment. I am right on track. Each moment in my life is a lesson and a prompt. What happens to me may be out of my control but I do control my response. As I am conscious of my current situation I am prompted to evaluate how to respond, what steps to take, and from what actions to refrain. I could allow myself to feel pressured by others and their comparisons. I could feel rushed and act in a haphazard fashion making mistakes in my haste to "catch up". Surely, if I can act in my own time, at my own pace (as long as my pace is not being delayed due to fear or self-limiting beliefs), then my life will flow perfectly, calmly and in the right direction for me.

Nothing that is coming to me will pass me by. Nothing that is not for me will stay. The universe will ensure this. We must be conscious of our lives, our thoughts, our words and our actions. Do not forget that inaction is a decision also. We are where we are until we make the next move. Do not fear or dread where you are, do not criticise yourself for not being further down the line – ignore those other voices! Being aware of where we are in relation to where we want to be will guide us and inspire us to make the next move. There is no need for comparison to others. Remember we all move at different paces and so, we are where we need to be right now. We are right on track, for now. Try exercise 3 if you want to reassess your goals.

5 I DESERVE HAPPINESS, LOVE, RESPECT JOY AND PEACE

I do! And so do you! We are beautiful human beings with the capacity to love and be loved. We are unique. We are wonderfully and inexcusably individual. Being authentically ourselves means showing the world our hearts and our goodness through our actions, our words and our flaws as well as our strengths. We are never called upon to be perfect. We are called upon to be our best selves. To try to be positive in our interactions and thoughts. Raise our vibrations to elevations where happiness and joy reside, where no negativity and toxicity can enter. Where we show warmth and kindness purely by living our best lives.

We can expect happiness in our lives, just as others do. Love is our right just as others experience it. Our lives will be peaceful and filled with joy. Just as others' lives are. We demand respect just as we respect others. What other people are entitled to, so are we.

You are worthy and deserve love, respect, and kindness. Never settle for less. What does it tell you if a person is rude to you or cold and unloving? What does it make you feel when someone disregards you or ignores you when you speak? We all need to be seen, heard and acknowledged so when this is denied us for whatever reason, it hurts. It is worth considering the reasons for people's attitudes towards us. If you are disrespected, stop and explore the possible reasons for this disrespect. What has prompted it? Did you invite it through your words or actions? Do you need to repair a relationship? Is this disrespect just someone else's poor behaviour or attitude? Are they simply projecting onto you their deep dissatisfaction in their own lives?

When you discover the reason for the disrespect, you can act accordingly, from a place of love. There is no need for bitter, petty revenge. If a person is toxic towards you have the grace and sense to walk away and fill your life with joy and peace with other people. There is no reason for you to allow poor behaviour towards you. There is no reason to permit disrespect.

Surround yourself with positive people who motivate and inspire you; who build you up and support you. Criticism and cruelty from a person reveal a sadness within them which you do not need to tolerate. You can have empathy for them but you do not need to allow them access to you. Such a person is weak, and troubled in his or her own way. It is not your job to heal them, although being your authentic, loving self will guide them if they are open to learning. Let your example be visible to all, but shared only with those who appreciate you. There is no person in this world who can say that you do not deserve love, happiness, peace and joy. It is our right to live fulfilling and inspired lives.

6 I RENEW MY LOVE FOR MYSELF EACH DAY

I renew my love for myself each day, excited for what is to come. Just as I express gratitude for the good in my life each morning, I like to show myself some love and appreciation so that I start fresh and motivated and buoyed by a sense of courage and optimism. As I reflect inward, I can assess my mood and my needs. I can evaluate my strengths and my talents and understand which ones the day ahead may require. I am reminded, regularly, that patience is one strength I need to build. I recognise that it stems from an unhappiness with certain situations in my life and although my impatience and curt comments are unwelcome both to myself and the recipients, I listen to the message they send me. I need to remove myself from certain situations and when I cannot I need to pull on my resources to show kindness and acceptance and patience. I am, after all, still a work in progress! And no! I am not using that to excuse my poor behaviour!

Although I spot my flaws easily enough, it is my strengths and good qualities I wish to notice and praise. I can validate myself without needing to hear flattery from others. (Compliments are always lovely to hear but I do not *need* them in order to feel worthy.) Knowing that my progress is continuing and that I am moving forward in my life, chasing my goals at my own pace and with confidence growing each day, encourages me. My motivation builds. I am aware that my self-validation can, at times, push me to work too hard, or do too much, or fail to see when I need to rest. This is where I need to love myself in a different way.

The term self-love is used regularly, but do we know what it means? I have learned that it means to take care of myself, to love myself by looking after my wellbeing. I regularly overdo things and work too hard and take care of everyone and everything until I am forced to stop. As I have said before if you do not take time for your wellness, you will be obliged to make time for your illness. You cannot pour from an empty cup. Self-love is vital. So how can we love ourselves better to ensure our wellness?

Each day do one thing that is purely for you – a bath, a walk in nature, read a book in a quiet space, go to the gym. Each week set yourself a slightly bigger reward – a massage, a day out, lunch or dinner with a friend, maybe. Each month you allow yourself something even more rewarding – an overnight stay away, a challenge like climbing a mountain (yes – I have done that too!) travel to a new place to explore. The rewards do not need to be financially onerous they just need to be all about YOU. They need to be something that brings you peace, joy, rest, recovery, relaxation (ok, maybe climbing a mountain doesn't achieve all of that!) and happiness. It is like having a reset button so you can let everything go. Allow the pressures of the day, week, month slip off your shoulders, if only temporarily. With this reset, this coming back to my centre, to acknowledge my needs in the moment, I am caring about my wellbeing. I am loving myself and I am re-energising myself ready for what is to come. With this new energy I can find new excitement and verve to go for it, to face my challenges.

Try scheduling something for each day, each week and each month. Put aside a little money each week to help with costs but remember, it is about the time and space you give yourself not necessarily the amount of money you spend on yourself. You may notice that none of the rewards I mentioned involve objects or possessions. It is not about indulging in shopping. Material things do not feed your soul as plentifully as actions and experiences. Time to find space for your soul to breathe, ground yourself in nature and disconnect from technology and duties. Give yourself some freedom; you have earned it.

7 I LEARN FROM MY PAST

I learn from my past and look forward with deeper understanding and hope. The past has value. Do not discount its lessons just because we say looking forwards and not backwards is the more positive way in which to live your life. Looking back brings memories, both good and bad. Nostalgia is beautiful but repainting the past with rose-coloured glasses is a dangerous thing. When I look back at my past, a whole lot of it is missing. I have blocked out so many memories subconsciously, in order to not re-traumatise myself or in order to just be able to move forward positively and not dwell in pain and a victim mentality. The past is done. The past cannot be undone. The consequences of the past are here. How I respond to past events and their consequences is my choice. Partly consciously and partly, as I have said, unconsciously. I know, that with hypnotherapy, I could unblock certain memories and deal with them. I could soothe my wounds with time-line regression and I could nurture my sad, injured inner child. I am working on this through meditation and quiet reflection rather than through hypnotherapy as I am able to do this myself, but a therapist is a helpful way to regulate tough emotions as you navigate your past.

The past should not control your present or future by locking you in a state of fear. Past traumas should be in the past and not carried forwards to punish and hurt your present and future. You deserve freedom from those wounds. Working through pain does not negate the trauma but simply releases you from the hurt and frees you to live life without reacting to triggers. I find that the work is an ongoing matter for me with some issues. I feel healed and then, bam! Suddenly something will trigger an emotional response from me and I will be shocked at its power. I take time to stop and reflect what happened and what it is bringing forward for me. Once I am able to trace the pain, I can sit with it and comfort myself. I allow the hurt and I metaphorically hug myself; Show myself compassion and love. I do not sit in self-pity as that is an unhelpful place to dwell. Nobody heals in self-pity; you merely allow the hurt and pain to define you and trap you in negativity. There is no glory in this. There is no progress or journey to freedom.

Knowing that I have survived certain incidents or situations in my life empowers me to know that I will survive anything that comes my way. Hopefully, I will not face more traumas but life is unpredictable despite precautions. I know that I have the strength, resilience and self-belief that will get me through any tough times. Knowing that I have survived (more than once before), tells me I will survive again. This is how the past teaches me. I draw on my inner strength, and other resources, such as confidence and courage and empathy, and I get myself through the situation facing me. Knowing who I have been teaches me who I am and encourages me to be who I am destined to be.

Where I used to be vulnerable to manipulators and clever narcissists, I am now wiser and protect my heart. Some may say that I have become cynical or closed off to love; there is truth in this to some extent. However, a small amount of skepticism or cynicism may be what I need in order to not trust blindly. I guard my heart until I am sure it is a safe space in which to love openly. I truly advocate loving with your heart fully open, it is a wonderful experience when it is with someone who deserves you. I just learned that I need to take my time to ensure that the person is worthy of my love, my time, my trust, because when you let someone in, you become vulnerable. In vulnerability lies true love and connection with another. However, in vulnerability lies the chance to get hurt – again. Past lessons are there to guide you, not to rule you or shut you down but to give you some guidance. I love myself and want to be loved in a way that makes me feel safe, cherished and valuable. Too often, I have been too needy of validation through relationships that I made poor decisions. Now, I look and listen carefully, with past lessons as a guide, and with a deeper understanding of who I am, what I want and what I deserve, I make wiser, better decisions. One of the most powerful messages I learned and repeated to myself as a mantra in my healing days I share with you now – "I stopped giving discounts when I realised my worth". It is vital that we see ourselves as loving and loveable beings. We must learn who we are and what we need and deserve. We must understand what we want and what we will not tolerate.

Do not settle – there is no settling to be done when you are trusting your heart and soul to another. If they do not deserve you, walk away. There is power in being alone, knowing your worth. It is not about pride; it is about loving yourself so much that only when you are truly valued do you choose to share your precious self with another.

8 I LISTEN TO MY EMOTIONS

I listen to my emotions and am curious to their source and purpose. Education allows us to expand our limited knowledge on various subjects and we can become skilled and learned about many things in life. One thing we are not taught, however, is how to manage our emotions. Parents and caregivers are our first teachers and some, unfortunately, did not graduate from parenting school! When a child has parents or caregivers who are regulated, (know how to manage their emotions and responses) they become regulated children and adults. If one of their parents is dysregulated, they too will be dysregulated as children learn behaviours they witness. That means to say that when an adult exhibits anger and aggression in moments of stress or difficulty, the child will adapt in this manner also. If a child sees an adult manage stressful situations calmly and mindfully, the child will learn to calm himself or herself, regulate their emotional reaction and will become a regulated adult. Do not forget that children do not have the pre-frontal cortex to help regulate emotions and impulsive behaviours until the age of twenty-one, so we cannot expect children to act as adults but they can learn how to manage their feelings as best they can, until then, if we give them healthy examples to follow.

Our thoughts stem from our emotions. We sense the world around us – through sight, sound, touch, taste or smell. The messages our brains receive though these senses are then filtered through our previous experiences and belief systems. This then leads us to our emotional response, both physically and spiritually. If I smell crayons or plasticine, I am immediately transported to my primary school classroom, I feel nostalgic and happy as those smells are associated with that period of my life. When I hear certain songs on the radio I am brought to tears through my association with that song in a particular moment of my life. My memories are brought forward or maybe just the feelings associated with the memory I have blocked away. I then have to wonder why this emotional response has occurred. Where does this sadness come from? What trauma or hurt has it brought to the surface?

If I feel angry yet don't know why exactly I will sit and ask myself what I am angry about? Where do I feel that anger in my body? How is the emotion affecting me physically. Sometimes it is a frustration rather than anger; sometimes it is sadness that has gone unnoticed or unaddressed for too long. It may be in my throat, choking me or in my chest like a heavy weight. Anxiety churning in my stomach, swirling and turning fast. By stopping and being with the emotion and checking in with my body to see how I am being affected gives me time to withdraw from the moment and focus on myself. What do I need right now. Air, space, calm, self-love, acceptance. It can be obvious what has upset me and the reason behind the emotional response. Then it is easy to address it and soothe myself appropriately. Other times, I need more time to understand what I am experiencing and what my body is asking for. There is always a message to hear.

It is common for people to criticise themselves for reacting emotionally and they apologise and are embarrassed. Emotion is normal, it is healthy, it is vital. Learn to listen to your feelings and the physical sensations that accompany the emotions. What can you learn about yourself in this moment. If you can listen to yourself, you may uncover a deep hurt which you need to heal. A past wound that feels neglected and overlooked. Take time to pay yourself attention and love yourself with compassion. Talking with a trusted friend or a therapist may help you to manage your emotions or accept past situations and alleviate the pain if you cannot do this by yourself. It takes time to learn how to unlearn dysregulated behaviours so do not belittle yourself. Be kind to yourself as you would to another person.

RISE

1 ENVISAGE YOURSELF LIVING YOUR DREAM LIFE

Imagine your dream life, the home, the people around you, the career, the abundance, the happiness. What do you want? Truly see it, feel it, desire it and believe in it. Make it happen, step by step. As you see yourself living that dream, it will seem more and more real and achievable. if someone else has already achieved your dream - so can you. So often we tell ourselves we could never do this or that, become a doctor or film director or astronaut - we tell ourselves only certain people can do those things - we are not connected enough or rich enough - stop coming up with excuses! Anyone who truly wants to do something will do it! It may take time, effort and perseverance but if anyone has already achieved what you would love for yourself then you, too, are capable of achieving it! Map out the steps you need to get there and work consistently, manifest and strive for that goal. Nothing is given that is worth having.

The definition of courage is stepping towards your goal *despite* the uncertainty. What's stopping you? Truly ask yourself this question. What do you want and what is stopping you from having it? Break down all the excuses you give yourself and you will see that the only thing holding you back is you. Your lack of faith in yourself. Your lack of belief in yourself. Your lack of courage in yourself. Nobody is born lacking in these things. Unfortunately, somewhere along your journey you allowed these qualities to dwindle, to fade. Perhaps, somebody told you that you were not clever enough or charismatic enough, beautiful enough, motivated enough, you just were not enough. Unfortunately, you believed them. Unfortunately, you gave their words and opinions power. Unfortunately, you allowed these destructive individuals the power to undermine and diminish you. Well, *that's* enough! We all make mistakes, but it is how we learn from them that defines us. Nobody else gets to dictate who you become.

Find your courage – even if it is merely a flickering glimmer in the darkness right now. You will add oxygen to your fire and soon you will glow with the confidence to attain your dream. Nobody gets to limit you – *you* certainly do not! It is time now, one way or the other, to move forward towards your goal, towards your dream, towards what makes you happy and filled with purpose. Write down what makes you happy – what you desire – what you want to achieve. However, it is imperative that you do not get confused with the destructive mindset of "I'll be happy when..." This is your shadow side fooling you and holding you back. How many times have you said, or heard said by others, "I'll be happy when...I lose weight, buy that house, I get engaged, I have children, I earn six figures…" Never put your happiness in this sort of frame. You can be happy right now with what you have and how you look, material things and uncertain futures are not the key to your happiness. You are your key to your happiness. Never put your happiness in the hands of another either. "I'll be happy when he proposes!" What if he never does? Do you spend your life on tenterhooks, never quite happy but living in desperate hope and uncertainty? I feel pain just imagining this scenario.

So, write down genuine goals which you truly believe will make you happy. Of course, some of your goals may be materialistic – but frame it differently. I, personally, want a big, comfortable home, in France, with a pool and plenty of space and grounds near the sea. Not because I am greedy or ostentatious but because I see my future with my children and their partners, I see my business expanding into retreats abroad in an atmosphere of tranquility and bliss. My property is not my status symbol but my home, my sanctuary for myself and my family; It is my source of income too. My goal is not shallow or superficial. It is not a pipe dream. It is a goal I am working towards, step by step. I realise I have lots to learn along the way and I will embrace it all. I am not relying on the achievement of this goal to give me my happiness – I am happy working towards it already. Achieving it will be the icing on the cake and the cherry on top!

So, step by step you too, can work towards your dream. Frame it positively, believing in your goal and in your ability to achieve it. Know that it is yours to attain, when the time is right, it will all fall into place – as long as you take steps towards it – take action and be positive. Nothing happens if you do not act. Nothing is given, but your efforts will be rewarded.

2 IT IS NOT NECESSARY TO BE UNDERSTOOD

It is not necessary to be understood - not everyone has the capacity to understand you. Not everyone will understand your journey. That's ok, it's not their journey, it's yours. This is about you. Only you will feel the changes, feel the need to change; only you will be urged to move in a different direction. The awareness that you gain may disarm others – their lack of comprehension is not your concern. Stay focused on your own journey and if they are open to their own awakening they may be inspired by what they witness happening with you. Do not worry about them. Do not feel obliged to explain or demonstrate or excuse anything. This is your journey for your own development, for your growth, your unlimited future. It is not selfish to follow your heart and soul towards a better future. It is not self-centred to focus on your own needs. It is not egotistical to insist on boundaries.

The more you learn on your journey of development the more you will realise that you need to limit some people's access to you. Some people bring negative energy and can wear you down. They suck your energy, your personality and your positivity until you realise you have nothing left. These energy vampires need to be removed from your life or at least you need to put boundaries in place in order to limit their access to you. You must protect yourself at all times. You are gaining strength and confidence with each day but you are vulnerable at times, for personal growth, facing your inner demons, can be painful and difficult. These toxic people may take advantage of you or diminish you in your weaker moments. Be careful and look after yourself, your space and environment. Flowers struggle to grow in a desert but change their environment to one of sun, rain and nurturing soil, they flourish. Find your nurturing environment, nourish yourself with healthy, balanced connections; People who cherish your growth, support you and encourage you to always be your best self. Stay close to people who feel like sunshine.

Avoid those who love to gossip and tear others down. People who delight in others' difficulties are hurting inside and can only find relief in belittling others to make themselves look better. It is sad and a sign of an empty and sad soul. Show them another way to be. If you cannot remove yourself from their draining presence show them how to not engage in character defamation and how to brighten their outlook on life with a positive light.

However, not everyone is open to new perspectives or enlightenment so do not despair if you cannot help them. It is not your responsibility to change anyone but yourself. Focus purely on how you want to live your life, the positive lens you wish to view life through, the kindness and compassion you want to nurture, for yourself and others. Those who mock you do not deserve access to you. Those who question you may be open to learning, however, so it is for you to discern if their curiosity comes from a place of genuine care or simply a passive aggressive way to ridicule what they do not understand. Remember people fear what they do not understand. They belittle it and deride it in order to not feel small as they stand ignorant before it. Smile, and move on. Do not forget that those that matter don't mind and those that mind, don't matter[7]. Keep moving forwards, do not look backwards; just smile and keep learning and growing. Their stagnancy is not your concern, just as your journey is not theirs.

---

[7] Bernard Baruch

3 THIS IS MY LIFE UNLIMITED – TO LIVE MY WAY

What are you waiting for? Permission?! This is *your* life – live it *your* way. Everybody has an opinion. It is up to you how much weight you give to those opinions. Do you live your life the way your parents tell you to? The way your friends think you should? Do you do as your teachers suggested? Yes, everybody has an opinion. So do you. Is your opinion truly your own or are you persuaded and swayed by others until you cannot trust your own decisions? Do you stand firm in your decisions, holding your dreams and beliefs firm?

If I gave up on my hopes and dreams because my family or friends derided or belittled them, I felt lost and small; insignificant and incapable.; as though my own feelings, beliefs or dreams were not to be trusted or satisfied. They were unworthy, wrong. I was taught to distrust myself. In time, however, my confidence has grown. I have learned to listen to my own voice. To realise one very important fact. This is MY life. All of these other people have their own lives to lead. Why do they get to dictate or manage my life too? I could not impose my will on others and in that same spirit I will no longer allow others to control my life. (When I have felt the urge to micromanage someone else's life I step back and ask myself why. It is usually because I feel the need to protect them from themselves. This is arrogant of me to think or act in this way – I am not here to "fix" others – they need to lead their own lives *their* way. I know my intentions are good but misguided and with this realization, I accept how others attempting to manage my life are also trying to be helpful and kind even if it is unwelcome.)

I have lived more than half of my life now so it is clearly time for me to take responsibility for my own life and my own happiness. By making more and more decisions for myself, choosing things to do, to keep, to discard, I began to trust myself. I am an intelligent woman who had been told for far too long that I was incapable, that I could not manage if others were not there deciding for me. Eventually the light shone for me and I could no longer live in the shade others cast. This is MY life. MINE. I get to choose – what I do, where I live, how I spend my money, how I raise my family. The freedom is addictive – it is too hard to relinquish it now. There is no reason to do so, though. I am not being selfish in realizing that this is my life. I do not live a life that denies other people's needs or desires; I care for my family and ensure their wellbeing, their security in my love. I do, however, realise now that my needs and my wellbeing are equally important, if not more so. If I have no joy, no peace, no happiness in myself, I cannot care effectively for those who need me. There is nothing to give. I cannot pour from an empty cup.

I have now learned to walk away from those who drain my cup. I take time for myself to feel calm again, to feel peace, to allow myself the space to do what makes me happy – to walk in nature, to read, to paddleboard, to tend to my garden, especially my roses. I am allowed to take time for myself. I do not need permission from anyone but myself. I shake off the guilt I used to feel, knowing how other people would judge me. Now their judgement means nothing. Getting to know my needs and how to show myself love and self-care I have begun to recognise how important I am.

I care for myself so that I am able to care for others. I live my life my way to enable me to confirm each day that I trust myself and I respect myself to know my worth. I live my life the way I choose now. The word "should" has been removed from my vocabulary as it implies somebody else's opinion. I know how to live my life, I know my goals, my dreams and I am learning how to attain them. I am free to choose my dream and take steps towards achieving it. I am free to choose the path I take - I am proof that you are never too old to start again! I hear the opinions of others, I hear their doubts, their mockery but now, none of that can dissuade me. They can live their life but this one is mine. I have earned the right to lead it as I see fit. The further I continue with my journey of growing my confidence and self-trust the more admiration I hear in people's voices and the less doubt, as though they are witnessing the changes and are respectful of my strength. I may make mistakes but that's ok. They are mine to make. They are mine to resolve. Mistakes are nothing more than opportunities to learn and improve. My word, have I improved over the years!

4 I CHOOSE PEACE OVER POINTLESS BATTLES

Pause before responding. Reacting is an unconscious act but to pause, reflect and then respond is the consciousness and awareness of a calm, high vibrational soul. Remember that your actions show your true self. Words are easy but following through with actions that show you care is priceless. When your actions align with your words, when you act the way you say you will, people can trust you. People can have faith in you and believe that you are a safe person to have in their lives. If, however, you say all the right things, repeatedly, but never come through with the goods, you never fulfil your promises, never do what you say you will – eventually people will see right through you. They will be disappointed and saddened but they will walk away. Eventually, there will be no more chances, no more excuses, no more pandering.

Those you have supported in this way only to end up disappointed and hurt need to work on themselves. They cannot rely on you or others to fix them. The individual who takes no personal responsibility for their own lives are children looking for a mother or a babysitter or a free ride. The caring souls who give endlessly, seeking to soothe these people give too much and get hurt or used. It is not a reflection of them that these people are such takers. Their low vibrational behaviour is a reflection of *their* own dark souls. Their inner sadness, their need. It is not for the empaths to fix or soothe. We try. We try too hard and for too long. But we need to learn when to walk away.

I do still say we should support others who may need us – show kindness when we can. The world needs kindness more than it needs us to be right. However, we do need to protect ourselves from being drained of our energy and our spirit. I have been drained by too many people who promised to do the work yet did not have the awareness or ability to fulfil their promises. It would be easy and I could be justified to argue my point against these people. I could give countless reasons for being angry or hurt. I could provide evidence for my disappointment and I could argue that I am owed an apology. Yes, I could do all of those things; But what would I gain? What does the argument give me? Do I feel I have won? Is my hurt diminished by being right? Does revenge wipe the tears away? Does holding a grudge hurt the other person? No. No to all of that. Would you go to the person who hurt you and ask for an explanation? Even if they had the emotional awareness to be able to explain their actions, it is unlikely that they would care enough to do so. Surely, you have just presented them with another opportunity to hurt you afresh. Your healing starts with walking away, head held high. Give no more oxygen to this fire.

Step away from pointless arguments and fights which only serve to prolong discomfort, unhappiness and bitter resentments. Seeking to prove your point, chastise the perpetrator, hurt them in return, merely continues the hurt, fuels it, keeps it alive gnawing away at you. Nobody wins in this manner. Is it about winning and losing though? Are there winners? If so, I would imagine it is the person whose soul reclaims their peace and stays calm and unbothered. A person who feels love and compassion rather than anger and scorn or contempt. I am confident in my truth and confident enough to not need to defend it. I can walk away from pointless battles and reclaim my inner peace. I have nothing to prove. What others think of me, if they should imagine that they have hurt me and "won", let them think that. I know my truth. That is all I need. My integrity is all I need.

Kindness and love can chip away at the cold bitter soul and help them find the light which warms them. Now that you have awareness and peace it is a blessing to share with others. You can lift them out of their shadows with your gentle warmth and openness. You can lead by example. Do not demonstrate this through victimhood, however. Remember, sometimes the only way to protect yourself in truth, is to walk away in silence.

5 FORGIVENESS FOR OTHERS IS A GIFT TO MYSELF

"You can complain about your situation or you can change it". Charlie Farley.

"Either you go after the life you want or you settle for the life you get". "Soul Vibes"

Accept it, change it or leave it – complaining is just a waste of energy. Everyone we meet in life is either a lesson or a blessing or both. There are no coincidences – we meet people for a reason. They are guided to us so that either they can help us or teach us something important, a life lesson to support our development as sentient beings; Or, indeed, so that we may help them.

Each of us impacts upon other people every day of our lives. Whether this is consciously or otherwise, we affect other people's moods, the events in their lives, their perspectives. Share a smile with a stranger as you walk down the street and you will perhaps receive a smile in return. Of course, there are cynical, miserable people in the world who will question your motives and look away but most people will meet your gaze and smile back. You lift their spirits, boost their morale, make them feel happy, even if just momentarily, with this one small gesture.

Undoubtedly, we affect others' lives in greater ways also. Sometimes we hurt people, damage them, just as has been done to us. If hurt is caused intentionally then we must question the motives behind that. What is hurting the perpetrator so deeply that they feel compelled to pass on that hurt? Passing on joy and happiness, positivity and lightness is a privilege. To witness the impact of your kindness is beauty itself. Yet how do we forgive those who pass on unhappiness, scorn, unhelpful gossip and pain? How do we forgive people who break our hearts?

Do we not feel entitled to exact revenge upon those who we see as intentionally hurting us? Do we not believe that we should do something in return for their cruelty? Why should we let them "get away with it"? Are they getting away with it though? I am heavily motivated by justice and equality, by fairness, so I will always have a strong emotion when I feel that there has been injustice served. However, I have learned to pause and step back from the emotions and review the situation calmly and as rationally as I can, with the emotions that I am experiencing. Some emotions will be because of the current situation but some will be old wounds brought to the surface by the current situation. I must check myself before I respond to the present moment by separating it from my past. If the hurt I feel is authentically related to the current situation I will need to deal with it.

I am not a vengeful person and will not seek low vibrational tactics to deliver karma. I will step back, put in boundaries and protection for myself and withdraw from that person or situation which has caused me pain. This is a response in itself and it can cause the original perpetrator hurt as they are not getting that emotional, dramatic, high dopamine rush from creating the fight. Step away, head held high. A person such as the perpetrator does not merit my time or attention. I will process my emotions privately. I would never go to the person who hurt me to ask them to justify why they did it. I will never hand them the opportunity to hurt me all over again! I will deny them the pleasure of thinking they have beaten me. However, as I write this, I am considering whether their opinion actually matters anyway? I do not need to justify my position, nor do I have to explain it to the person who hurt me. They do not deserve my explanation. They deserve to see me walk away living my best life. Being positive and successful is my best "revenge".

One more important factor to consider as you remove yourself from the person or place that hurt you. Forgiveness. Not because they deserve it but because you do. Anger and bitterness eat you from the inside. They take up residence in your thoughts and in your attitude and in your face. Do you really want to hurt yourself on top of the hurt they caused you? I need to release those negative feelings and thoughts. They drag me down and steal my inner peace and happiness. That is not how I want to live. I need to forgive them and move on with not a single thought for them. I did not deserve to be hurt by them; I do not deserve to linger in pain so I set myself free by letting go of anger towards them. I change my view of the person and their behaviour. There is always a reason behind a person's behaviour – a hurt or damage they carry with them. With curiosity, I can *try* to understand. Maybe they are wounded and not sufficiently emotionally intelligent to have the self-awareness to have healed or to behave better. Hopefully, one day they will have that awakening but until they do I show them compassion, let them go and release myself from caring or hating. I feel the blessing of release, they do not even need to know. The forgiveness is for me, not them.

6 STARS CAN'T SHINE WITHOUT DARKNESS

Be open to whatever comes next. Find what makes your heart sing. Find what gives you purpose and fulfillment. When you are living the life you are meant to be living, your soul sings. Never settle, aim higher and strive for true happiness. Who knows what path you will take but whatever you do – take a path- don't just sit still, waiting for life to happen to you – Go! Make it happen… your way! Oh, and don't worry – you can switch paths as often as you need until you find your true calling – in your own time. There is no right or wrong way – just go one way… or the other. Either is better! Just keep on going, step by step.

Each day is a new day so do not waste time worrying about what has gone. Today is a fresh chance to do better, to be better. Be brave. Step forward and embrace this new opportunity.

Do not be afraid. Life will present you with so many twists and turns, obstacles and joys. Some we can expect and others will surprise us. Some events in our lives will bless us and others will torture us and just as people are either blessings or lessons, or both – so too are the events we face. We can choose to protect ourselves by hiding away and living little, insignificant existences or we can open up to a whole world of vibrancy and experiences, both negative and positive. We can open our hearts with curiosity and hope and step forward with courage and optimism. If we fear change and the unknown, we will never find the joys that await us. If we are too scared to open the doors, we will never find the opportunities. Yes, life can be hard and so painful. I know this only too well. Yet, I refuse to give up. I refuse to quit, my life is mine to fill with joy. I will not allow the negative people who want to bring me toxicity to hinder my progress or dim my light. In the pain I have experienced I feel my sparkle diminish but I know that in time I will find my way back to glowing with love and kindness in my heart, despite the ugly side of life I have faced.

Stars can't shine without darkness.[8] I choose to shine.

I choose to live differently. I am open to what is next all the while, working towards my goals. What is meant for me will never pass me by. What is not meant for me will not materialise. I take my aim and live with optimism and positivity. If I live with integrity, I will succeed. Therefore, I ask you to try life in a different way, with peace and optimism in your soul. Take each day as the fresh opportunity that it is – a gift – and make the most of it. Revel in it and benefit to the fullest. Grab each chance, embrace each exciting uncertainty and see where it may lead you.

---

[8] Wayne Mustaffa, 2016

Take action towards your dreams and find your peace. Never fear, be excited.

7 SELF-HEALING

The sadness of lost "could have beens", "should have beens", the loss of hopes and dreams and expectations is powerful. Feeling cheated and bereft feeling so hurt and sad – it is loss – that is the hole that needs filling.

How do you fill that emptiness? This hole is the invitation to addiction. People start to look for soothing and it can be found in many ways although not all are helpful, ultimately causing more issues and pain long term. Addiction is the result of a disconnection, an emptiness and sense of solitude and feeling unsafe. Johann Hari[9] writes in his book *"Lost connections: Why you're depressed and how to find hope"* of how disconnection prompts people to self soothe in ways a person with healthy relationships and fulfilling life would never consider. It is Hari's TedX Talk on addiction that opened my eyes to the human condition and our fragile

---

[9] Johann Hari; *Lost connections: Why you're depressed and how to find hope*

souls.

A healthy life is one that is filled with friendship, a true solid social group, hobbies, fulfilling work and a sense of purpose. These are key ingredients for a life free of addiction. If one of these is lacking, if we have no connection to other human souls, we search for soothing.

The simplest, fastest and most promoted method of soothing is alcohol. Have you ever questioned the way society pushes alcohol as the answer to everything? Had a stressful day? – Have a drink; Had a good day – celebrate - have a drink! Got engaged? Married? Promoted? Won the lottery – have a drink! Funeral – drink, wedding – drink, romantic date – drink, Baby born – drink! Apparently, parenthood can only be survived with the liberal use of alcohol – "Mums need gin", "It's wine o'clock", "It's 5 o'clock somewhere!" How sad that encouraged alcoholism is just another meme these days.

It is infuriating how alcohol is pushed and promoted when governments know only too well that it causes cancer, addictions, liver diseases, obesity and mental health issues. Cigarettes were eventually acknowledged as carcinogenic and harmful. Packets are now sold with strong messages, visual and written, to attempt to dissuade the user from their harmful habit. No such plan exists as yet, in The UK as far as I am aware, although labels on wine bottles in Italy created a lot of unrest within the wine industry recently. Alcohol sales still provide huge revenue for governments. It also keeps people suppressed and malleable.

Alcohol is pushed, promoted, lauded and praised. It is all wrapped up in pretty packaging and marketed with clever words. When you strip all that away you are being encouraged to drink ethanol – a poison – a fuel for your car! How tempting is that? It is tempting because the hole is there – the aching need is there. The dark sadness a disconnected person seeks to escape, to numb, to ignore.

That first sip, that first glass eases the initial stress and tension. However, scientific research shows that with the second drink the anxiety not only returns but it grows.

I used to drink wine. I was a connoisseur, I worked in a French chateau, I studied and gained wine tasting qualifications. I knew my wine – I was a wine snob. However, eventually when life took a dark turn, I used wine to numb my heartache, my sadness, my lost "could have beens". The end of my marriage set me free but allowed me to acknowledge the hurt of twenty years of being cheated: He was never the best friend I dreamed of, he was not the amazing father I wanted for my children, he was not the support and connection I needed. He left me lonely in my marriage, isolated, struggling with my disappointment. Striving to find happiness in a marriage where only one of us tried. My dreams were destroyed, my hopes were crushed. It hurt.

I still occasionally feel the loss of what "should have been", yet without my experience I would not have become the person I am today. That does not advocate his behaviour, nor excuse it. I am simply acknowledging the strength I gained through surviving the heartache.

I have found that a sad, disconnected soul can heal. Old friends, old habits, all gone. I left the toxic behind and sought out truthful, heartfelt, genuine connections. My life today is so very different from my married life. I have fulfilment in my children's lives and their love; in my career as a hypnotherapist; in my authentic friendships – some old and genuine from the start and so many new friends. I am blessed and I express my gratitude daily. I removed alcohol from my life – it slowed me down and held me back, it limited me. But no more! My life is now open, free and without limits – hence the name of my hypnotherapy practice – Life Unlimited Hypnotherapy. We deserve so much more than we allow ourselves in our small lives. Open your eyes and see the horizons to aspire to. Rise up and feel how good life can be. Find the friendships, the true people, find yourself – who you are behind every mask you have ever worn. Find what, where and who makes you happy. There will be no dark hole of loneliness needing to be filled with sex, alcohol, gambling, shopping, smoking, vaping, drugs or social media. These transient, empty solutions just bring more problems with them. The initial buzz or soothing they initially provide is destroyed by the eternal addictive need they create long term. You drink to soothe the anxiety, then you're anxious because you need a drink, so you drink to soothe the anxiety the lack of drink created. A vicious loop to escape.

Find another way to soothe yourself. Walk in nature, paint, write – journaling is a great way to allow your feelings out and to feel a release – sometimes with free-writing (just letting your thoughts flow naturally without overthinking); go paddleboarding, kayaking, walking, exercising, running, studying, reading, trying something completely outside of your comfort zone – join a group – open up your environment to new possibilities and new friendships. The world is vast and so too, are the opportunities we can find once we are open to receiving them.

8 LEARNING SELF-AWARENESS IS AN UNPARALLELED FREEDOM

"Yesterday I was clever and wanted to change the world – today I am wise and I am changing myself". *Anon.*

Understanding yourself is a lifelong journey of discovery as clichéd as this sounds. I know myself better than I have ever done as a younger woman. It is as though I needed to endure my traumas and hardships as well as my joys and successes in order to become the woman I am today. I have learned, through experience and through the studying that I felt compelled to pursue, who I have been, what I endured, what I participated in, what I needed to accept, change, forgive, forget or remember. I have learned who I am today, what my strengths are and what my weaknesses are. I know what I need to work on and I have the beginnings of understanding how to do that. I am a work in progress.

Sometimes in order to learn who you are it is helpful to travel alone. To strip back all the distractions and noise around you. To be open to self-reflection. To seeing your true self, flaws as well as strengths. Being alone is not lonely when you learn to love and accept yourself. Never forget to keep learning, open your eyes and your heart to new concepts, adventures and miracles. Life is exciting and special when you can remain open and receptive. There is so much joy, happiness, excitement and knowledge available to all who remain curious and willing. That is a skill in itself, for we have spent so many years behind walls and self-imposed barriers, to protect ourselves. Break free from those self-limiting obstacles and take a risk.

It is never too late to start again, to start something new, something that scares but excites you; a new hobby, a new career, a new course of study, entering into a new source of friends – a new social group or setting. We find it difficult in this age to make new friends. Where do you go as a twenty year old? A thirty five year old? A forty something year old? Dating apps met a need but polluted it. Friendship apps, unfortunately, have also been tainted by those with poor low vibrational intentions. Yet, we still need to step out of our comfort zone and try something different. It is the definition of insanity according to Einstein, to keep doing the same thing and hoping for a different result. So, what new thing can you try? One small change?

Seek out your soul tribe, your kindred spirits. Align yourself with those who match your energy, your morals, your beliefs and core values. By actively participating in what you love – paddleboarding, book clubs, working out at the gym – you will encounter like-minded people. Engage in conversation, openly and receptively. Find who your spirit glows beside. You will know when you simply feel happy around them –

no doubts about how worthy you are, no comparisons regarding beauty, ability or otherwise. You will just feel at ease and peaceful. You will feel that you can be yourself in all your splendid weirdness. You are heard, accepted, welcomed, appreciated, valued. If your new social friends give you all of this, reciprocate – it will come effortlessly, as the ease of being with similar people is soothing and reassuring.

Learn about yourself first, and foremost. Write down what matters most to you. Do you place a higher value on money or friendship? Is family important to you? Do material things matter more than a healthy social life? How about your moral code? Is honesty and being genuine vital to you or could you be friends with someone who is less truthful when it suits them? You must know yourself before you choose your crowd. Be the person who shines as the example rather than the one who follows. Choose people who you admire and who inspire you – for the right reasons. They will motivate you to be your best self. Their example will encourage you to shine and strive for better in all areas of your life.

Remember, there is always time and opportunity to grow and learn and to become even better. Never settle. Never quit. Never abandon hope. There is so much more to life. So many exciting moments to experience, so much friendship and love to feel. Life is too short to sit passively as it drifts by. Be brave, be hopeful, be authentically you and welcome all that is yours. Take one step forward, open your heart, smile and go for it. Life is yours to truly enjoy. No more existing – live! Live life fully and with the curiosity and excitement of a child not knowing what is coming next but ready to embrace it wholeheartedly. Never stop becoming you.

We are all a work in progress.

PART TWO

12 PRACTICAL TOOLS

1. The Circle of Control

Starting at the beginning of everything – let us define what it is we need to concern ourselves with. Do we worry about things unnecessarily? Undoubtedly! We are conditioned in so many ways throughout our lives, to care about what other people think or say about us. Are we responsible for everyone and their feelings, thoughts, beliefs? Or, just our own?

Look at the circle below. Consider carefully what you think should fit inside the circle and what remains outside of the circle – things that you control, things that you cannot control. Once you have completed your version, compare it with the circle of control I completed. Do you agree or disagree?

Out of my Control

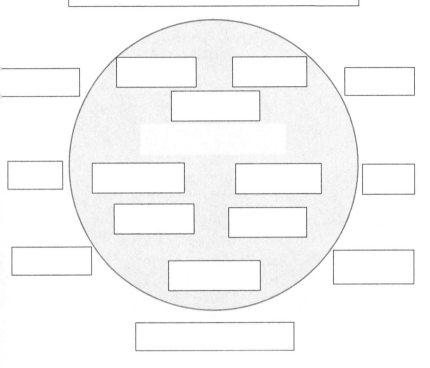

So much of what worries us is actually outside of our control. We cannot change, manipulate or create an outcome – some things are just not within our control – and that is ok. The hardest thing is for us to allow it to be, to accept it and to remain calm and not let it affect us.

Stoicism is a philosophy dating back to early 3rd Century in Greece and Rome. The Stoics encouraged us to recognise what lies within and outside of our control and to focus only on what we can control such as our thoughts, our emotions, our words and actions. In allowing all else simply to be and not concerning ourselves with the actions of other people, we find a peace that is so rewarding.

What has happened in the past cannot be changed; regret serves very little purpose. It can cause us distress and guilt so how can it bring us peace? Acceptance and allowing yourself to learn lessons from what has been, is far more beneficial.

The future is coming but we cannot unduly influence it – we can prepare as best we can but to truly believe we can control every aspect of the unknown is narcissistic in the extreme. Leave anxiety to the side and be curious as to what will happen, how events will play out. Be prepared and careful but fear not what will come your way. What is yours will never pass you by. If it is not the right path for you, it will not come to fruition. You will manage all that comes your way, challenges included.

The people we surround ourselves with is a big factor in who we become[10]. Choose wise, motivated, purposeful people; People who have love and gratitude in their hearts, who choose to live positively and unlimited by bad habits or negativity. If you spend your time with heavy drinkers or smokers, chances are you will also take up these habits. If

---

[10] Jim Rohn, motivational speaker. Motivational speaker Jim Rohn famously said that we are the average of the five people with whom we spend the most time.

you choose to socialise with self-starters, enthusiastic, motivated, health-orientated people, you are more likely to experiment with healthy lifestyle changes and become encouraged to step outside of your comfort zone in a positive way.

Far too often, we concern ourselves with what other people say about us or think about us. We give their opinion too much importance, as though, their opinion is a definition of who we are and how much we are worth. Nobody knows you as well as you do. Act in ways that are true to you, in ways that make you proud of yourself, happy with your words and thoughts and actions. Your response is what you control – not the actions or words of other people. How you respond to them shows who you truly are.

In order to behave in a calm, positive and respectful manner we need to be conscious of what we consume, what we allow to influence us daily. Although what we consume physically as in food and drink, is, of course, important in terms of our self-care and self-love our daily diet of social media, trash TV, overload of depressing and catastrophizing newsfeed has far more power on our mindset and inner peace than we, perhaps, realise.

Choose wisely, just as with the people you surround yourself with, filter your daily intake from external sources. Think carefully about the language you use in your own head about yourself. Do you criticise every silly mistake, do you call yourself names when you drive the wrong way, forget something, give the wrong answer? Do you stop and allow yourself to be human? Do you stop and consider if you would ever speak to another person in the same way? Think about your inner voice and self-talk – we will come back to this in chapter 5.

2. The Wheel of Life

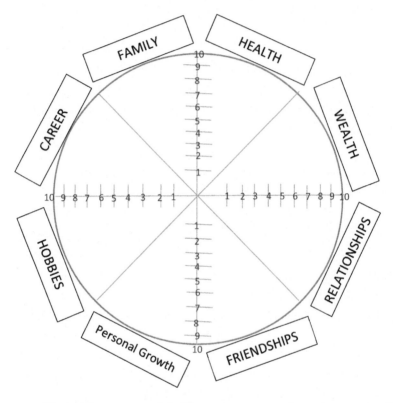

If you have ever felt like you are stuck and unsure of what to do; Or, that you don't even know what's wrong with you but you just don't feel right - *Things* don't feel right; If you have ever felt that you are just not happy but can't quite put your finger on what exactly is the matter, then the Wheel of Life is a great tool to help you identify areas of your life to work on. Life needs to feel balanced and we need to satisfy many different areas of our soul, even those of which we have not yet become aware.

The first Wheel of Life resource here has been given headings pertaining to different areas of life. Each section is marked with numbers 1- 10 to allow you to quantify how content you are currently with that specific area of your life. For example, if all is going well with family life, you may highlight a point at the 8,9 or even 10 marker. If your social life has been miserable and empty and you feel as though you lack solid connections with friends whom you can trust, you may mark this section with a low score. Please continue to reflect honestly and evaluate your current level of happiness with each section that you deem important. Use the given headings or adapt as necessary. For example, each section could be an aspect pertaining to your career, or relationship.

When you have placed all the markers, draw a line connecting each segment around the circle. The evidence will highlight which areas of your life currently needs attention. This helps to focus your efforts and set goals that will truly benefit you. Be grateful for the areas that are going well. Can you identify reasons for the success in those areas? Perhaps, you have skills or learned lessons that you could use to transfer across to the less successful area? Make a note by each section to justify the grade you gave. As you come back to this wheel in a week or two, you will be able to look back and see what has or has not changed. Paying attention to the actions you take and their effects will guide you further. Maybe what you did did not improve matters, so let this guide you to a different approach. If it worked, could that same tactic work in a different area of your life?

(Remember, you can return to this regularly, as life shifts constantly and what may be going well today may falter later and require your attention). Set goals accordingly.

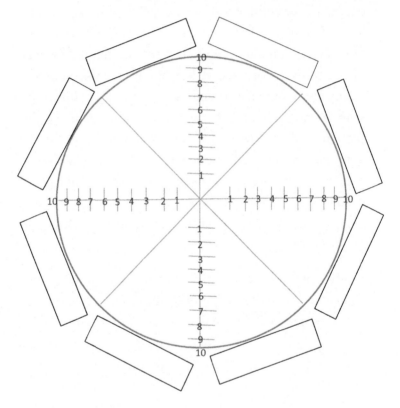

3. Setting Goals

Setting goals is a complete unknown quantity for so many of us who have not grown up with the knowledge that we are autonomous and have a choice in how our lives turn out. Yes, it's true – you can be whatever you want to be! If someone else has already done something, then there is no reason as to why you should not also achieve that goal. It is not all about who you know, or how wealthy your family is. A lot of it is self-belief. Have a dream and take steps towards it – even if they are simply small steps – one step forward is still progress. No action, no step taken, is stagnation, procrastination and disappointment. So, take the positive step towards your dream.

Having first established what area of your life you want to focus on by using the Wheel of Life you can look at how to set a goal – obviously, a goal or dream should be realistically achievable. It would be pointless to aim to become the King of England when you are a 20 year old woman, living in Texas, with no family ties to the Royal Family in England. So, what makes a goal achievable?

There are many acronyms and ways to set a goal. SMART[11] goals are what we will use for this instance.

---

[11] Doran, G.T. (1981) There's a SMART Way to Write Management's Goals and Objectives. Journal of Management Review, 70, 35-36. - References - Scientific Research Publishing.

Specific – be detailed and precise – use clean language to state your goal.

Measurable – will you be able to clearly see progress / goal achievement?

Attainable – is this within the realms of possibility?

Relevant – is this worthwhile? Appropriate at this time?

Time-bound – you have a completion date in mind.

Anxiety and depression can occur for people who do not feel they have a purpose in life. Many of us carry out duties and jobs, which do not inspire or enthrall us. They offer no fulfilment as such and this can lead to a sense of purposelessness. Feeling inadequate, uninteresting, unworthy. Surely, there's more to life than this? Right?

So, what is your heart drawn towards? What inspires you? Ignites you with a desire to act and achieve? Sometimes, it takes years to discover one's sense of purpose. For some, it comes naturally. Until we know what our true purpose in life is, we have the joy of being curious and to explore. Try different things, in different places, with different people. Remember – choose wisely the people with whom you surround yourself!

If a major life-changing goal seems too much right now, set yourself a smaller, more accessible target for now. Build on each success and build your self-confidence and self-worth until you are ready to take that leap.

Look at the SMART worksheet below and complete it for your goal. Ask yourself the questions and be honest and realistic in your answers.

SMART Goal Worksheet

S.M.A.R.T. Questions...

Specific   Does your goal clearly and specifically state what you are trying to achieve? If your goal is particularly large or grandiose, try breaking it down into smaller, specific SMART goals.

Measurable How will you (and others) know if you are making progress on achieving your goal? Can you quantify your outcome?

Attainable   Is achieving your goal dependent on anyone else? Is it possible to reframe your goal so it only depends on you and not others? What factors may prevent you from accomplishing your goal?

Relevant   Why is achieving this goal important to you? What values in your life does this goal reflect? What effect will achieving your goal have on your life or on others?

Time-bound When will you reach your goal? Again, if your goal is particularly large, try breaking it down into smaller goals with appropriate incremental deadlines.

Today's Date: _____ **Date** by which you plan
to achieve your goal: _____

What is your goal in one sentence?

_____

_____

_____

The benefits of achieving this goal will be...

_____

_____

_____

Specific: What exactly will you accomplish?

_____

_____

_____

Measurable: How will you (and others) know when you
have reached your goal?

_____

_____

_____

Attainable: Is attaining this goal realistic with effort and
commitment? Do you have the resources to achieve this
goal? If not, how will you get them?

_____

_____

_____

Relevant: Why is this goal important to you? Focus in on why it matters.

_____

_____

_____

_____

Time-bound: When will you achieve this goal?

_____

_____

_____

4. Choose your Path

Are you a confident decision maker? Do you make decisions rashly or procrastinate and fail to reach a decision? Do you research and get yourself fully informed before deciding or do you get advice from everybody you meet? There are times where we may behave in any of these ways because we may find decision-making easy or difficult at different stages in our lives.

One way to choose between two options is to use a strategy from Neuro-Linguistic Programming[12] - Timelines – This is where you visualise yourself having made a decision. You have two options and imagine two separate timeline paths. Choose the first path for option A, as though you have fully committed to this decision and as you physically walk down the timeline path you see yourself having arrived at a future date maybe 1 or 5 years from today. Turn round to face the direction from which you have walked. When you see and feel yourself at this future date having made and committed to this decision A through to completion.

How do you feel having reached this point in your life? Are you filled with joy? Peace, satisfaction? Dread, unease? Excited? Relieved? Peaceful? Anxious? Disappointed?

Return to your starting point and walk down the second path for option B, until you reach 1 year or 5 years after committing to this decision. Turn around and look back at

---

[12] Neuro-Linguistic programming, Richard Bandler and John Grinder

where you came from. How do you feel having reached this point in your life? Are you filled with joy? Peace, satisfaction? Dread, unease? Excited? Relieved? Peaceful? Anxious? Disappointed?

Return to your starting point in present day and compare the feelings and emotions you experienced on both journeys. It may be very clear that one decision left you feeling much more positive than the other. Occasionally, neither pathway is clearly the "one" so perhaps it is back to square one and search again for alternative options, although this timeline pathway travel does generally leave you with a clear intuitive feeling of what to do next.

5. Rid Yourself of Negative Self-Talk

How often have you called yourself an idiot or stupid or clumsy or insulted your physical appearance? It is so common to insult yourself when you make a mistake. However, it is NOT justified! We criticise ourselves, consider ourselves worthless, not good enough, too fat, too thin, ugly, inadequate. How is it so much easier to believe the criticisms and insults that we, and other people, say and so difficult to accept the compliments? The beliefs we grow up with, the social conditioning we receive, the media we consume – all feed into our negative image of ourselves. We don't match the model thinness in magazines or on social media, we aren't millionaires by the age of 19 on YouTube, we live mundane lives, day to day. Even in our mundane lives we doubt ourselves, comparing ourselves with others – believing everyone else has their life together, know what they are doing and are happy. I'm going to break it to you – they don't have it all sorted, they're just as confused, unhappy and lost as you are. Of course, there are people who have done the work and who are on the way to finding their peace and happiness. So, you can too. Never look at somebody and assume anything. Everyone is hurting from something in their lives. We all have a story. We are all dealing with life. Nobody is better or worse than anyone else. Read that again!

The negative voice we hear can be our own voice or an echo of a controlling parent or teacher or grandparent. An action or thought triggers a memory of what they would say in that circumstance and instantly you feel bad, worthless, insecure, or sad. Whose beliefs are controlling your thoughts here? Imagine the next time that you swear at yourself, insult yourself, criticise yourself for something, that you are saying those exact words to your friend. Would you *ever* speak those words to a friend? Would you? Chances are you would never be so cruel. So why would you be so cruel to yourself? You deserve love, affection and acceptance from yourself just as you would give to your friend. Be your own friend, not your bitter enemy.

Remove the voice!

Exercise:

Whether the voice is yours or a parents' voice criticising you it is no longer welcome. Your head holds space now for purely positive affirmations and reassurances. Take the negative voice and transfer it out of your head to your thumb nail. Hold out your hand far from you and see the voice, or even the face of your critic, in that nail. Repeat the negative phrase from your nail to your face but imagine the speech in the voice of Mickey Mouse or a robot or any silly voice that makes you laugh. It sounds ridiculous – it has no power, no validity. It's simply a joke. It cannot hurt you. Now flip it off your thumb into the distance. It is no longer welcome; it is not needed anymore.

Perhaps, the negative voice brings with it a visual scene that you recall, an unhappy memory. The face of your bully, the scene of unhappiness. The beauty of the visual image is that you can freeze frame it. STOP! You catch the critic with their mouth wide open criticising you. How ugly and silly they look caught in that moment! Take a second to witness their ridiculousness. Laugh at them – you cannot take them seriously in this frame. However, we no longer want to remember the scene or words. The freeze frame muted the sound, reduced the person to a visual joke and now you can drain the image of all colour down to black and white and fading fast. Now imagine yourself screwing up the paper this image is on and throwing it far, far away, or even setting it on fire. No way is that image coming back to haunt you now. That negative voice has been ejected.

When you take something away something else comes in to replace it – it is up to you what you allow to replace that negativity. It is up to you to choose how you speak to yourself. It happens quite quickly, (if you are conscious of this) that you can stop the habitual negative criticism and replace it with a kinder acceptance. We all make mistakes; we do not need to be emotionally hurt because of it. I would often call myself an idiot or a moron (words I heard in my marriage, unfortunately) if I dropped something or broke something or forgot to do a task.

Soon enough I learned to be kinder to myself and say "whoopsadaisy" or "oh that was silly", "oh, never mind, let's fix that now." I am human; humans make mistakes. It is normal and not the end of the world so learn to stop catastrophizing silly things, be patient with yourself, and others, and believe me, you smile a whole lot more, especially when you catch yourself saying "whoopsadaisy"!

Using positive affirmations is another way to fill the void but the way in which you frame those affirmations is crucial. Let's look at this in chapter 6.

6. Meet yourself with Compassion and Acceptance

I have yet to meet a perfect human being. I do not even know what a perfect person would look like. Do you? Physically, humans are drawn to one another and yet we do not all desire the same people, so there must be a reason for that. If there were such a thing as a perfect person then only those people who were genetically created in that way would be desirable and the rest of us would only want to be with them. However, we see men and women of all different shapes and sizes, race and colour, hairstyles and heights. Many of whom are in loving relationships. Therefore, I like to believe that there is someone for everyone! Perfect does not exist, unless reframed as "perfect for me".

However, the media we consume, the insults we hear, the judgments made, all serve to twist our perspectives. We start to see ourselves as not thin enough, not pretty enough, not clever enough, just not enough, too loud, too lively, too demanding, just too much. Who says? Who is telling you that you are not enough? Or, too much? Stop! You are perfect as you are. Sure, there are things we can work on to be our better selves – personally, I still need to work on my patience! Generally, however, we need to look at ourselves with kindness, compassion and ultimately, acceptance.

I am riddled (or rather, blessed) with stretch marks after having children. I used to hate this about my body. I was ashamed and felt ugly. Eventually, with the help and love from others, I began to see these scars as beautiful testament to the power of my body, creating and birthing four healthy children. I have recently gained weight and am struggling with this new shape but I am trying to be kind to myself and accept that with age and different stages of my life, I will look and feel differently. Different but not worse. Worse implies a comparison and comparison is the thief of all joy![13]

We are born into this world perfect. Even those with a disability are perfect. We are as we are meant to be. Our parents love us instantly and as we cry at birth, we know that we will be loved and cared for and our needs will be met. It is only as time passes and people let us down or disappoint us that we start to see ourselves as less than worthy, less than perfect. We feel hurt and rejected and we attach reasons for that abandonment. Whether it is told to us or we assume, we start to look at ourselves less than favourably. As though we are no longer good enough, we are lacking or failing in some way. The assumption is that we are at fault somehow. We know, however, that we are more than some people deserve, we just need to remember our worth and only offer our love to those who recognise our true value. We value ourselves – we do not need somebody else to validate us.

Just as I reframed my stretch marks from scars to trophies, we can reframe our positive self-talk. There is no point in looking at myself in the mirror and saying I am perfect and have a beautiful body. My mind would reject that (although that shows my personal wounds). I can, however, state affirmatively that I am beautiful and working towards a

---

[13] Theodore Roosevelt

healthier and fitter body. This is true and undeniable (for we are all beautiful). My unconscious mind will accept this. I can say, "I am becoming more courageous each day", "I am working on becoming more patient". Stating that I already am patient would be false and falsehoods would be rejected so I choose the phrasing carefully, positive but truthful. Whatever I am, or want to be, I AM enough[14]. I am me. I am worthy of love, affection, compassion and acknowledgment. First and foremost from myself. Once I truly love and accept myself, perfectly imperfect[15], working towards my highest self, I no longer seek validation externally. Of course, I love compliments and love as much as the next person, but I do not need to lower my standards or disrespect myself in order to attain those.

Exercise:

Find a comfortable, quiet place to sit alone and allow your thoughts to go inside.

Think about yourself and allow thoughts to pop in. Possibly, they will start as negative thoughts about your physical appearance or your success or your personality traits. Allow these thoughts to come through and kindly, with self-love, challenge each negative thought calmly. Be curious as to why you think that negative thought about yourself. Who planted the belief originally? Can you grant yourself more compassion and acceptance? Can you see that you are beautiful in your unique way? Accept yourself as you are; be compassionate and forgiving if you find faults. If these faults

---

[14] Marisa Peer, *I am enough*.
[15] Brené Brown, *The gifts of imperfection*

are something that you want to amend, visualise yourself working on that aspect and ultimately, living life with the improved qualities. If the changes you want are physical, set yourself SMART goals (exercise to help you attain your ideal change. Be realistic and kind. Do not succumb to dark thoughts where the only way to improve yourself relies upon plastic surgery or other extreme measures. If you do find things you would like to improve about yourself aim to improve those areas without damning yourself for your humanity. Remember, we are always a work in progress.

7. Courage and Curiosity

Being vulnerable is difficult. Most people struggle to open up to another person with their true feelings, raw emotion, life stories, hopes, dreams, failures. Mostly we keep these close to ourselves, only opening up occasionally when we begin to trust another and feel secure enough to do so. The success or failure of relationships depends partly on the level of communication between partners. Sometimes we even find it hard to be truthful to ourselves. We fool ourselves into believing that everything is ok, we're happy. Opening our eyes and being curious, looking for the truth scares us for we do not know if we will cope with what we discover about ourselves, our relationships, our lives.

We have a choice in how we approach life. We can remain closed and defensive, protecting ourselves from being hurt or we can open our hearts, stay curious and therefore, ready to experience life in all its potential glory. Yes, this does make us vulnerable but it is the only way in which we can welcome new people, experiences, knowledge and love into our lives. If doors remain closed we will never access the joy (or pain) on the other side.

Exercise:

Find a cool, quiet place to sit alone with no distractions. Find a comfortable position, sitting or lying down, if you prefer. Close your eyes, if you feel safe to do so and take a few deep breaths in through the nose and slowly out through the mouth. Once you allow your breathing to settle back into its natural rhythm you can feel how your heartbeat has slowed and calmed and you are ready to listen to your inner wisdom.

State in your mind, or aloud if you prefer, "I am opening my heart. I am allowing myself to be curious about life and myself. I allow myself to feel love and joy and open myself to living life fully, unlimited by fear."

Allow thoughts to enter your mind and be curious. If you feel fear, ask yourself what scares you? Ask yourself "What do I fear would happen if I remain open?"

Sit quietly, and listen to the thoughts that come to you in this quiet reflection. This is an exercise to repeat regularly and as it becomes more familiar and comfortable with practice you may find answers come quicker and fear recedes. You allow yourself to remain open, not defensive and closed off, but truly open to experience life in all its colours.

You may find moments when you feel truly open and excited but suddenly fearful of getting hurt, like you may have experienced before. You shut down and close off, defensive. Breathe. Listen to the fear, trace it to where it came from originally. Seek to understand it. Allow it a moment but then remind yourself that this moment is not the same as that moment in the past. The people in your life are not those of your past. Do not attach old wounds to new people.

Yet, be aware of your intuition, your inner guidance. There may be something to pay attention to in this moment. Allow your heart to guide you – not through fear but through a wisdom you have but that you may not yet be aware of. Congratulate yourself for finding the courage to become open, even if only briefly. You can try again and it will be easier now because you have already learned how to be courageous and curious. Keep practising, keep praising yourself, keep trusting yourself and keep being brave.

8. Step into your Power

Each of us is individually blessed with skills, talents, and unique personalities. As we become dragged down by self-doubt and criticism, self-lead or through insults from others, we forget just how wonderfully special we are. We forget our strengths and powers. We forget that we were blessed at birth and we need to retrieve our forgotten strengths in order to live our lives unlimited.

We have all achieved something in our lives, no matter how old or young we are. We have all survived something, conquered a fear, completed a challenge. Perhaps, it is simply that we do not take time to acknowledge our successes. Perhaps, we do not even recognise them as successes. Do we ever celebrate our wins, our accomplishments, however small or insignificant they may seem?

It is time to recognise ourselves with curiosity, compassion, and acceptance. Look within ourselves to recall occasions when we have shown strength and power, resilience and courage. Finding and recognising those occasions when we have exhibited those skills and resources allows us to acknowledge what we are capable of and we harness those resources to carry us through our next challenge. For this, we use anchors.

An anchor is a positive trigger. It helps you recall positive emotions which give you the powerful memory and recreates the same strength of a past moment for you to use in the present moment.

I am about to step on stage to make a presentation to 300 people. I could allow nerves and self-doubt to overcome me. I could allow my legs to shake and my voice to wobble. My mouth might go dry and I may stumble with my words or even forget what I am supposed to say. Or, I could set myself an anchor to give me the strength, the courage and the self-belief I need in this moment to do a fantastic performance.

It is clear which outcome is preferable. So, how do we avoid the first outcome and achieve our successful presentation instead?

We look at what resources we need – courage – self-belief – confidence – inner strength.

How do we get these? We get these vital ingredients from within ourselves. We have already done things in the past where we have been brave or shown confidence, where we believed in ourselves; where we overcame nerves and succeeded. These may come from one specific incident or from several different moments. It does not matter. We know that we have experienced all these things before, so we stand up, we close our eyes and we recall the scene. We feel the same pride, confidence, strength, self-belief etc. that we had in that moment. We build it up, expanding and increasing the strength of the memory and the emotion.

At the very peak of the emotion, we step forward into an imaginary circle of power. This circle is the first anchor we set.

Bearing in mind the emotions we are trying to anchor we may choose a colour of power, strength, victory – for me that colour is red. It may be different for you so choose what works best for yourself.

Bring forth those memories, the intense feelings once more and step into that circle of power in your chosen colour. You are surrounded, protected and energised by this colour combined with the emotion recalled by the memory.

Your second anchor may be a physical one – to prompt instant recall of the powerful feelings you need to experience. You may choose to clap your hands together, or slap your hand on your leg as you step forward; you may clench your fists or click your fingers – choose your own physical action as your anchor.

You may have realised now that anchors are best sourced via our senses – we are reminded, triggered or anchored via taste, touch, sounds, smells and sight. I can smell children's crayons and be back in my primary school classroom. Or I smell my favourite perfume and feel confident and attractive. Anchor whatever makes you feel the emotions you need such as strong and confident through your own personal senses. Wear your favourite scent, listen or imagine hearing your favourite power song, wear your lucky tie or dress; Link that colour with your circle of power. With so many positive empowering anchors you cannot fail to succeed.

So, at the moment you need to harness these resources you need to fire off the anchors. The memories of these empowering emotions will flood you and stay with you when you recreate the anchors, fire them off one by one, hear the song, smell the scent, see that scene of your previous success, step into your coloured circle of power and clap your hands.

These anchors can be taken from the same or different occasions that generate the positive resources you need. They are your personal references and will work much more powerfully if you find them yourself rather than taking other people's suggestions.

Exercise:

Imagine a circle on the floor in front of you. What resource do you need right now? Do you need courage? Do you need to feel capable? Do you need resilience or inner calm? Choose a colour that represents that emotion for you and fill the circle with that colour. Turn up the colour as bright and vividly as you want. For example, let's say you want to feel brave enough to give a presentation to your superiors at work. What colour inspires or represents courage for you? I choose red as it is my colour of power.

Close your eyes and recall an occasion in your life when you felt courageous. What bravery have you shown? When did you need to be brave, and calm? Recreate that scene in your mind. When you feel the confidence and courage from that memory create an anchor (a way to trigger a response – like attaching a physical reminder) that you can use to relive these emotions. I tend to clench my fists by my side but you may choose to clasp your hands together or slap your hip or any other physical action. Some people hold crystals or another object that fills them with courage or strength. Some people carry a lucky pen or wear a lucky suit – these are examples of resourceful anchors that some people choose to use.

Replay the scene, and when you feel your chest fill with that courage you experienced back in that moment step confidently into the "red" circle on the floor. Lift your head, clench your fists* and step into your power. Repeat this action with the combined actions anchoring the sense of courage, confidence and powerful calm several times so that when, in the future occasion, you need to feel calm, confident and resilient, all you need to do is step forward into your circle of power, imagining the "red", clasping your hands,* seeing and feeling yourself as you want to be.

The beauty of the circle of power is that you can use it to recall any resourceful strength you need – courage, confidence, calmness etc. for any occasion. You create your own visual, physical and even olfactory (smell) anchor to help bring your inner powers forward in the moment you need them.

*(Or do whatever physical anchor you prefer)

9. A New Perspective

Do you believe there is only one way to look at a situation? I doubt that. It is very easy, however, to get stuck with a single thought or in tunnel vision where you cannot find the answer to the problem. Sometimes our relationships start to flounder when we argue and resolutely fail to compromise or to understand other people's points of view. Using Neuro-Linguistic Programming's Perceptual Positions[16] helps us to open our minds and hearts to alternatives. There are more ways to view a situation.

First position – your own personal point of view

Second position – the other person's point of view

Third position – an outsider's neutral point of view

You can continue to explore further if you choose with

Fourth position – the community's point of view (Business / society / club)

Fifth position – a spiritual point of view (whichever faith you choose)

---

[16] Neuro-Linguistic Programming, Richard Bandler and John Grinder

Exercise:

Physically stand up and consider the problem / situation which concerns you from *your* point of view – state aloud in the *first* person how you feel about it. "*I* think…, *I* feel… *I* see … *I* want… / don't want … etc.)

Move one step to your right and step into the second position – comment on the situation from the other person's point of view. "*I* think…, *I* feel… *I* see … *I* want… / don't want … etc.)

Move one step to your right and into the third position – the outsider's point of view looking in. "I think…, I feel… I see … I want… / don't want … etc.)

Continue with 4th and 5th positions if you choose – how does your company / society, club see the situation and the consider how the situation would be viewed by your faith.

Once you have spoken from each position return to the first position and see if you continue to view the situation in exactly the same way as before the exercise or if perhaps, you have been enlightened in any way from the other perspectives. You may have changed your original point of view, or perhaps not, but by allowing yourself to consider other perspectives you open your heart and mind and curiosity can enable better communication and understanding which support better relationships.

10. An Attitude of Gratitude

Inner peace is *not* impossible to achieve. A bold statement, I know, but when we understand what creates inner peace you will soon agree with me. Life is not always calm or without its tribulations but we can still feel peaceful, or at least access that peace within us during mediation or moments of quiet stillness. If you view life as negative, focusing on the difficulties, the pain and the drama you will need to shift your perspective in order to access peace. The easiest way to achieve this is to be grateful. Whilst life is difficult and challenges will always arrive at your door, there is always some reason to be grateful.

My first moment of gratitude each day is to find myself living and having a new day given to me. I am grateful for the opportunities ahead, whether they are easy or difficult. The tricky challenges allow me to use my brain, my wits, my experience. It demands my full attention and self-control. I am grateful for my intellect and my emotional awareness which I have enhanced through recent years of emotional traumas and personal growth and study. I am grateful that I can be the support that others need. I am grateful to be fulfilling my purpose in life. I am grateful for the sun, the rain. I am grateful for the beauty in nature. I am grateful for my family, my true friends, the lessons I have learned through my false friends also.

There is gratitude for everything. It is a choice as to how you view the world. It is true that sometimes it is almost impossible to find a positive in the darkness and I have experienced this recently through a difficult bout of illness. I lost my voice when I caught Covid and I could not make a sound for seven weeks. Nothing! As a teacher and as a hypnotherapist my voice is my tool. I am nothing without my voice. Having discovered nodules in my throat I had expressed fears that I would lose my voice and wondered how I would cope. Ironically, a couple of weeks later I found myself in this exact situation. I was lost. It was a dark, scary and sad time. I lost my identity, I felt worthless; I felt guilty at letting my students down just as their exams approached. I could not find gratitude for a long time. Then something shifted. I began to view this as a lesson I needed to learn.

I am not good at sitting still or doing nothing. I recognise that I feel worthy purely if I achieve, create, produce or do something. My validation is to prove myself of use, and worthy. I was hard on myself for failing my students, for putting extra strain on my colleagues, for being emotional at home with my family, struggling with the darkness of being mute. I had to view this from a different perspective. I listened to other people. I read and found ways to relax. Serendipitously I came across the same message in several different formats in one week. Clearly meant for me to see.

Silent = Listen

I was being told to listen. Stop talking (forced to do so with vocal cord damage) so I could listen instead. I watched and paid attention to my environment, to other people, to signs and synchronicities. I had, once again, forgotten how to relax and recover, how to live a balanced life. I need rest as much as any other person but I do not often afford myself that luxury, feeling somehow inadequate.

"If you do not focus on your wellness, you will be forced to focus on your illness."[17] I understand now. Ironically, I am now grateful for what has happened to me. I am still struggling with pain and discomfort and a weak, odd-sounding voice, but it is finally returning and I can, once again, join short conversations. My gratitude lies in being forced to take time out to recover. I would never take time off work unless forced to and even then, I would rush back as soon as I could. That decision was taken from my hands and I cried. Then gratitude arrived with my understanding and acceptance of what had befallen me and why. I am grateful for the time to recover and regain my strength, to be patient with the vocal cords and learning to speak properly again. Forcing my voice could cause long term damage. I cannot afford to risk that and so I have learned to put myself first. I am grateful for the support from my school in looking for ways to help me return to work and not struggle.

Unfortunately, my recovery has faltered and a return to work inevitably undid all the progress made. My voice failed me again. Teaching is not the environment in which to heal right now, it seems. A message is being given to me yet again – I must LISTEN.

---

[17] Joyce Sunada

Exercise:

At least once a day, stop whatever you are doing, wherever you are, and list three things for which you are grateful. There are many journals on the market to encourage you to do this in the morning as you journal at the start of the day and to repeat at the end of the day. If you are like me and find it hard to establish and maintain the journaling routine in the morning, forgive yourself and do this instead. It is more spontaneous and authentic to find yourself suddenly overwhelmed with a feeling of gratitude. I feel utter joy when I experience this attitude of gratitude. It is not just happiness but a higher level altogether. Joy at having wonderful people in my world, being able to pay the bills for myself and my family, for being loved, for being able to enjoy nature and take time to be still. There is so much to be grateful for and although the world is often a dark place that presents us with so much to fear, dislike or resent, I choose to focus on the positive as my life is brighter and lighter and blessed with positivity. I do not look at my job (which can be challenging at times) as a burden rather as a blessing – It's not that I *have* to do this but I *get* to do this - because I am blessed with the skills. I am fortunate. What do *you* choose to focus on? Try gratitude for a month and see how you can reframe your world and how much lighter your spirit feels.

11.   Neurological Levels

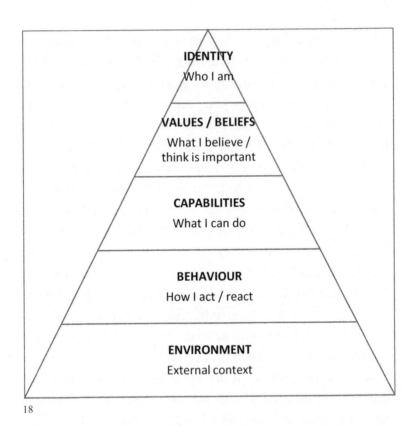

18

It is time to ask some big questions and look deeply within yourself.

---

[18] Robert Dilts

Who are you? At your very core – who are you? Have you ever asked yourself this question? Do you often reflect on the principles or morals you hold? The beliefs you hold? Do you ask yourself if you are limited by your surroundings? By the people in your life? Are you free to be your true self or do you have to adjust yourself to fit in?

You can apply these values and the questions they raise to evaluate if you are living your life unlimited or need to make changes. If you have a specific goal, or purpose, you can apply these questions towards that.

We start at the base of the triangle as without a safe solid foundation we cannot move further.

Environment is very simply the where, when and with whom something takes place. It is the "context". How do these elements impact upon you? Are you in the right environment to achieve your goal? Are you with the right people or do they hold you back? Are you ready to take action? Imagine your goal was to live a successful, healthy life and quit bad habits but you were currently living in a squat with drug using mates. How easy will it be for you to quit doing drugs and apply yourself to working every day? The environment, the people and the timing are all wrong. You will need to address this issue immediately.

Behaviours are what you actually do. Awareness of a person's behaviour guides us to understand that person better. So how do you act / react when faced with challenges? What is good about your reaction and what needs changing?

Capabilities refer to the skills, abilities, and qualities that you need. What can you do?", What are you capable of achieving? Do you need training in order to progress? Do you have the resources necessary?

Beliefs are ideas we hold as being true. Beliefs are what we think we can or cannot do. What we think is true, correctly or incorrectly. We acquire values and beliefs in early life also and they shape our decisions and actions. Are your beliefs valid and helpful? Are your beliefs misleading and distorting reality?

Values are what matters to us – our principles and the things that are important to us. We have unconscious filters in our mind, again acquired from childhood, which define for us what is "good", "moral", "worthy" ""important", "acceptable" or not. What is important to you? What really matters? What is a non-negotiable? Things like honesty, loyalty, authenticity etc

Identity: This is about how you see yourself, your sense of self, who you are. "Who am I?" At your core who are you? Are you a good person, someone who seeks to bring peace and support or are you a selfish person only thinking of your own needs at all times?

Purpose: This refers to your higher purpose. "Who or what am I doing this for?" or "What is my higher purpose in this context?"

When you are faced with a dilemma or need to find an answer to a situation an analytical approach step by step up the neurological levels may expose hidden elements which need addressing in order to find the resolution.

Exercise:

Use these questions to make notes and establish how your Neurological levels currently are:

We start at the bottom as our environment is where everything begins. If our starting point is not "safe" and grounded we are set up to fail. Each level needs to support us in our goal achievement.

Environment: Am I safe where I am? Am I in the right place? At the right time? Are the people I am with a positive or negative influence on me? Is this the right moment to start this goal or am I not ready? If the answers to these fundamental questions are positive, we can proceed up the levels.

Behaviours: How do I behave when faced with a certain situation? What behaviours do I need? Do I need to alter my approach?

Capabilities: Am I actually capable of achieving this goal right now? Do I need to learn any additional skills? Do I have the talents and abilities to proceed successfully?

Beliefs: Do I believe in myself? In my abilities? Do I believe that a person such as myself can reach this goal or do I have self-limiting beliefs which hold me back? If so, I need to work on these before I proceed.

Values: Do I actually agree with the goal or the manner in which I need to behave in order to achieve it? Do my values and morals align with what is being asked of me? Do I feel comfortable with this situation? Is this goal worthy?

Identity: If I proceed with this goal, do I see myself truly aligned with it? Is this who I am, truly? Am I representing the true me in this situation? If I am not, what do I do about it?

Purpose: Am I reaching for this goal because I believe in it and because it is my purpose? Will I feel good when I have achieved this?

If, at any stage your answers feel negative you are being asked to reflect deeper – on the issue at hand, on who you are and what you truly want and need from your life. Finding a true purpose which aligns with your goals, values and morals, which satisfies you and matches you in all senses is the way to inner peace and success in terms far greater than monetary.

Can you see an area of your life, a goal or situation where you could apply this deeper analysis? Step by step until you see the area which needs action or change. Remember, this is not about changing yourself to fit the situation always; It is about knowing whether you are in the right place doing what feels right and comfortable with you. Yes, stretch outside of your comfort zone but never deny your true values and beliefs. If you are being asked to set your principles aside by someone, question their motives. Question what it will cost you in the long term. Stand firm should any person or situation ask you to veer from your inner moral compass.

12. Banning "should"

This is my ultimate tool of liberation. It plays with chapters 5 and 6. Negative self-talk and negative self-image or self-worth all use the word "should".

"I should be thinner", "I should be better than this by now"; "I should have known that!" "I should be able to do this!" "I should be more like my sister".

Should? Who says? This one word implies a judgment. It implies someone else has put ideas or beliefs in your mind to steal your peace. Should implies comparison and I have said it before…Comparison is the thief of all joy.

What would change in your life if you removed the word "Should"?

Exercise:

Each time you instinctively say to yourself a sentence (– a criticism, let's be honest,) which includes the word "should" you need to

1. shout "STOP" at yourself.
2. Examine the sentence and see how truthful it is.
3. Where did this belief come from?
4. Reframe the sentence in the positive.

For example: "I should have known that answer!"

STOP!

Who says you should have known the answer? Is this true? Perhaps, you studied hard and on a good day, with less stress, you would have recalled the answer. On this occasion, however, it eluded you. That is human. Whether it is your voice or your teacher's voice – let it go.

Reframe the sentence.

"I knew that answer but it escaped me at this time."

Can you feel how much kinder this is? The world is a critical place – do we really need to add to it and criticise ourselves? Show some compassion to yourself.

The kinder we can be to ourselves, the kinder we are able to be to others. Learning compassion and kindness, gratitude and courage, our hearts can remain open and we can view the world from all its angles. We can learn about others and ourselves and we can choose to put ourselves in better situations with better people. We can balance our lives and listen to our hearts and intuition about what we need and what we do not need. We do not compare ourselves with others but focus on what we control, and with peace in our hearts, we let everything else be. We can be brave to set goals and take steps towards achieving them. We can make conscious, thoughtful decisions which move us forwards with confidence.

Each day is a fresh start and an opportunity to be better than yesterday. Take steps, day by day, with courage, joy and excited curiosity, just like a child. Life is too short to live in the dark, so let the light in.

I AM A WORK IN PROGRESS

ABOUT THE AUTHOR

Joe Quieros is a clinical hypnotherapist, coach, licensed NLP practitioner and counsellor registered with GHR. Joe is the founder of Life Unlimited Hypnotherapy. Prior to her training in hypnotherapy, she was a modern languages teacher teaching French and Spanish in secondary schools. Joe is a mother to 3 daughters and lives in Essex.

Printed in Great Britain
by Amazon